Gilles Paquet

Unusual Suspects

Essays on Social Learning Disabilities

Collaborative Decentred Metagovernance Series

This series of books is designed to define cumulatively the contours of collaborative decentred metagovernance. At this time, there is still no canonical version of this paradigm: it is *en émergence*. This series intends to be one of many 'construction sites' to experiment with various dimensions of an effective and practical version of this new approach.

Metagovernance is the art of combining different forms or styles of governance, experimented with in the private, public and social sectors, to ensure effective coordination when power, resources and information are widely distributed, and the governing is of necessity decentred and collaborative.

The series invites conceptual and practical contributions focused on different issue domains, policy fields, *causes célèbres*, functional processes, etc. to the extent that they contribute to sharpening the new apparatus associated with collaborative decentred metagovernance.

In the last few decades, there has been a need felt for a more sophisticated understanding of the governing of the private, public and social sectors: for less compartmentalization and sectors that have much in common; and for new conceptual tools to suggest new relevant questions and new ways to carry out the business of governing, by creatively recombining the tools of governance that have proven successful in all these sectors. These efforts have generated experiments that have been sufficiently rich and wide-ranging in the various laboratories to warrant efforts to pull together what we know at this stage.

The seventh book in the series probes some of the important reasons why social learning disabilities plague the Canadian socio-economy and in particular the public sector. It draws attention to the lack of critical thinking, crippled epistemologies, mental prisons, lack of *affectio societatis*, excessive politeness, political correctness, failure to confront, unreasonable accommodation and intellectual laziness as not unimportant parts of the problem. The depth of the Canadian *malaise* and potential ways out of this situation are explored.

Interested parties are invited to join the Chautauqua.

– Editorial Board

Other titles published by Invenire are listed at the end of this book.

Gilles Paquet

Unusual Suspects

Essays on Social Learning Disabilities

INVENIRE

Ottawa, Canada
2014

University of Ottawa **Press**
Les **Presses** de l'Université d'Ottawa

The University of Ottawa Press (UOP) is proud to be the oldest of the francophone university presses in Canada and the oldest bilingual university publisher in North America. Since 1936, UOP has been enriching intellectual and cultural discourse by producing peer-reviewed and award-winning books in the humanities and social sciences, in French and in English.

www.Press.uOttawa.ca

Library and Archives Canada Cataloguing in Publication

Title: Unusual suspects : essays on social learning disabilities / Gilles Paquet.
Names: Paquet, Gilles, author.
Series: Collaborative decentred metagovernance series.
Description: Series statement: Collaborative decentred metagovernance series | Reprint. Originally published: Ottawa, Canada : Invenire, 2014. | Includes bibliographical references.
Identifiers: Canadiana (print) 20220285365 | Canadiana (ebook) 20220285411 | ISBN 9780776638881 (softcover) | ISBN 9780776638898 (PDF) | ISBN 9780776638904 (EPUB)
Subjects: LCSH: Public administration—Philosophy. | LCSH: Public administration—Psychological aspects. | LCSH: Public administration—Canada. | LCSH: Social learning.
Classification: LCC JF1351 .P279 2022 | DDC 351.01/1—dc23

Legal Deposit: Library and Archives Canada, Third Quarter 2022
© University of Ottawa Press 2022, all rights reserved.

This book was initially published by Invenire Books in 2014 in the Collaborative Decentered Metagovernance Series. The cover design, layout and design were produced by Sandy Lynch. The University of Ottawa Press reissued this book thanks to the support of Ontario Creates.

Invenire

Invenire Books, an Ottawa-based idea factory that operated from 2010 to 2019, specialized in collaborative governance and stewardship. Invenire and its authors provide creative practical and stimulating responses to the challenges and opportunities faced by today's organizations. The list is now carried by the University of Ottawa Press.

Profession: Public Servant
The Entrepreneurial Effect: Practical Ideas from Your Own Virtual Board of Advisors
La flotte blanche : histoire de la compagnie de navigation du Richelieu et d'Ontario
Tableau d'avancement II : essais exploratoires sur la gouvernance d'un certain Canada français
The Entrepreneurial Effect: Waterloo
The Unimagined Canadian Capital: Challenges for the Federal Capital Region
The State in Transition: Challenges for Canadian Federalism
Cities as Crucibles: Reflections on Canada's Urban Future
Gouvernance communautaire : innovations dans le Canada français hors Québec
Through the Detox Prism: Exploring Organizational Failures and Design Responses
Cities and Languages: Governance and Policy – An International Symposium
Villes et langues : gouvernance et politiques – symposium international
Moderato Cantabile: Toward Principled Governance for Canada's Immigration Policy
Stewardship: Collaborative Decentred Metagovernance and Inquiring Systems
Challenges in Public Health Governance: The Canadian Experience
Innovation in Canada: Why We Need More and What We Must Do to Get It
Challenges of Minority Governments in Canada
Gouvernance corporative : une entrée en matières

Tackling Wicked Policy Problems: Equality, Diversity and Sustainability
50 ans de bilinguisme officiel : défis, analyses et témoignages
Unusual Suspects: Essays on Social Learning
Probing the Bureaucratic Mind: About Canadian Federal Executives
Tableau d'avancement III : pour une diaspora canadienne-française antifragile
Autour de Chantal Mouffe : le politique en conflit
Town and Crown: An Illustrated History of Canada's Capital
The Tainted-Blood Tragedy in Canada: A Cascade of Governance Failures
Intelligent Governance: A Prototype for Social Coordination
Driving the Fake Out of Public Administration: Detoxing HR in the Canadian Federal Public Sector
Tableau d'avancement IV : un Canada français à ré-inventer
A Future for Economics: More Encompassing, More Institutional, More Practical
Pasquinade in F : essais à rebrousse-poil
Building Bridges: Case Studies in Collaborative Governance in Canada
Scheming Virtuously: The Road to Collaborative Governance
A Lantern on the Bow: A History of the Science Council of Canada and its Contributions to the Science and Innovation Policy Debate
Fifty Years of Official Bilingualism: Challenges, Analyses and Testimonies
Irregular Governance: A Plea for Bold Organizational Experimentation
Pasquinade in E: Slaughtering Some Sacred Cows

The University of Ottawa Press gratefully acknowledges the support extended to its publishing list by the Government of Canada, the Canada Council for the Arts, the Ontario Arts Council, the Social Sciences and Humanities Research Council and the Canadian Federation for the Humanities and Social Sciences through the Awards to Scholarly Publications Program, and by the University of Ottawa.

ONTARIO ARTS COUNCIL
CONSEIL DES ARTS DE L'ONTARIO
an Ontario government agency
un organisme du gouvernement de l'Ontario

Canada Council   Conseil des arts
for the Arts   du Canada

Canadä

uOttawa

"Politeness is a way of not talking. When we are being polite, we say what we think we should say ... Politeness maintains the status quo."

– *Adam Kahane*

Table of Contents

PART III   On The Canadian Scene

| On Social Learning Disabilities

"... avoir raison n'est jamais une satisfaction ..."
Michel Déon

Preamble

This book is a sequel to another recent book I co-wrote with Ruth Hubbard on the bureaucratic mind in Canada, a book in which we reported on a number of safe-space conversations with some 100 senior executives of the Canadian federal government (Hubbard and Paquet 2014). From dozens of these conversations, we speculated on the reasons why such "conversations did not go deep enough ... to construct a way forward ... leaving a dangerous reality unaddressed and unaltered (Kahane 2004: 56-57)."

Adam Kahane, on the basis of his experience, might ascribe much of the disappointing results of these conversations to Canadian politeness. Ruth Hubbard and I were not as single-minded. We identified a variety of social learning disabilities that might, in part, be ascribable to politeness, but also to other flaws having to do with a twilight of critical thinking that echoes some debilitating aspects of Canadian culture: excessive politeness, political correctness, and a propensity to be unreasonably accommodating, to name but a few. As a result, much social learning is stunted and ineffective governance ensues.

Over the past 30 years, a social learning approach to problems of governance has become an important emerging perspective. It developed in response to a greater awareness that power, resources and information were widely distributed into many hands and heads, that no one was fully in charge in organizations any longer, and that there were no values shared by all the relevant stakeholders. In such a situation, organizations have to discover their goals and means through inquiring and social learning as experience unfolds, and as the traditional notion of top-down governing is replaced by collaborative co-governance.

The stylized notions of strategy and policy collapse into the notion of an inquiring system, and the notion of leadership dissolves into the notion of networks responsible for the stewardship function (Paquet 1999a, 2009; Paquet and Wilson 2011).

In this new emerging context, any impediment to effective social learning becomes toxic (whether it can be ascribed to learning disabilities by individuals or groups, or to blockages created by institutions and ideologies) for it entails impoverished stewardship and wayfinding for organizations, poor value adding, and insufficient innovation.

Much attention has been given to structural features, like centralization, as the sources of learning disabilities (Brafman and Beckstrom 2006; Kliener 2012). Much less attention has been given to the various sources of organizational failure that are ascribable to personal flaws and ideological biases – such as when individuals or groups continue to presume that problems can be approached as if they were well-structured *ab ovo*, as if goals were known and agreed to, and as if means-ends relationships were ascertainable and stable. Such flawed epistemological presumptions – that problems are benign and *not wicked* – constitute significant impediments to social learning very much as is the surreal worldview of governing that is based on those false premises. These simplifying presumptions are only crude devices to hide the fact that wicked policy problems cannot be handled by the traditional methods of analysis, and that new, more synoptic approaches have to be developed, both to probe those wicked problems and to design adequate arrangements to deal with them (Brown 2008).[1]

It is undeniable that centralization, a most important feature of the institutional order, appears to stall social learning. This has led to the proposal of various strategies of decentralization to improve social learning. However, other impediments have also been shown to be ascribable to the dynamic conservatism of interest groups whose welfare would be threatened by the change generated by social learning (Schön 1971). There is also much in the corporate culture or in the common public culture that may stall the operations of a learning organization: providing or failing to provide the *esprit de corps*, trust, and other ingredients underpinning effective coordination and collaboration. Some comparative sociological analyses have shown that different cultures impact significantly on the performance of organizations (Hampden-Turner and Trompenaars 1993).

Whatever importance one might ascribe to the structural factors and the institutional order in explaining the stunting of social learning, a significant portion of social learning failures remains ascribable to unusual suspects like cognitive, cultural and ideological blockages, interest groups, and personal factors that stunt the process of production of new knowledge. Social learning is mediated by individuals and groups, with traits that may significantly distort their perceptions and influence their capabilities and willingness to exert their intellectual capabilities to learn.

---

[1] The notion of wicked policy problems (goals either not known or very ambiguous, means-ends relationships poorly understood and highly uncertain, complexity of the issues such that the traditional analytical tools cannot handle them) has been developed in Horst W.J. Rittel and Melvin M. Webber (1973). See also Gilles Paquet (1999b).

A new twist to the entitlement mentality

This unwillingness to learn – that one observes in agents and groups, with their cultural, social and ideological blockages – deserves more attention.

In any modern socio-economy, a fair portion of the population works hard at value adding, while another group – wittingly or not, if not entirely parasitic – tends to shirk, and take advantage of a broadly generous system of redistribution of income and wealth, while not truly carrying their own weight. In the era before the welfare state, the latter group was composed of persons widely considered as deserving of help because they had been hit by all sorts of misfortunes for which they could not reasonably be held responsible. In recent times, this latter group has grown significantly; has based its claims on more and more problematic arguments; and has developed a sense of entitlement for whatever transfers they can possibly extract from the first group (Paquet 2013).

This entitlement mentality has attached itself not only to the hunger for financial benefits to compensate for disabilities of all sorts (real and imaginary), but it has now also permeated the process of acquisition of knowledge. A sense of *entitlement to effortless acquisition of knowledge* has also developed. This cognitive laziness has led too many to accept uncritically initial first impressions of the problems they encounter (that are often apt to be narrow and superficial) and to resist any invitation to reframe their perspective on these problems because it is cognitively too costly (Michalko 2012).

But it has also led a significant portion of the population to systematically shy away from trying to cope with anything hard to understand. The American novelist Thomas Pynchon reacted sharply to complaints by commentators about his novel *V*, who claimed that it was difficult to read and understand. He responded with a phrase that created a mini-scandal in the late 1970s, "Why should things be easy to understand?" This may be the best riposte to the growing entitlement to intellectual laziness, and to the refusal to exert the mental effort necessary for learning that has come to characterize a major segment of the population over the past 40 years.[2] Such a sharp denunciation of *le droit à la facilité*, and of the canonization of the 'law of no effort' is rarely heard in our world of complacency. That is why Pynchon's statement that there is no entitlement to have effortless access to new knowledge generated such an uproar.

In too many areas, a large number of pseudo-experts have begun to show signs of having ceased to be willing to exert themselves to learn. The same trait has been observed in cohorts of graduate students who want credentials without pain; and in the newer cohorts of public servants who have been anointed as executives, and have, perhaps, been overly celebrated as members of a new expert clergy, and seem to have forgotten that hard learning is expected from them.

Without the pressure of competition or the robust enforcement of standards, they have lost any sense that they need to continuously update their knowledge base as circumstances change if they are to live up to the imperatives of their burden of office. This is a phenomenon that was noted as early as in the 1940s by Harry Truman (a former president of the United States) who said it would appear that the experts around him could not learn, for if they could, it might then be concluded that they were not experts to begin with.

This reluctance to work hard at learning has also been notably observed in executive development programs for Canadian federal bureaucrats. While most of these programs were extremely demanding in earlier decades, and participants were willing to work very hard at developing new knowledge bases and skills in order to gain access to higher echelons of authority in the public service, many of these programs have more recently drifted into some form of easy-going-palavers-cum-show-and-tell-cum-tourism, leading to automatic 'graduation' without much intellectual effort ever being required or exerted.

---

[2] This was Thomas Pynchon's response to Jules Siegel (1977) about the complexity of *V.*

These changes resulted from participants having become more and more rebellious in the face of demanding courses, and having complained bitterly about exacting demands or tests. As a result, the standards of continuing education programs have been dramatically relaxed, and they are in danger of losing their legitimacy as a serious form of acquisition of knowledge.

In fact, it has come to be expected (except in the very restricted world of serious and robust professional training) that things should be easy to understand, and that, when serious intellectual efforts are required, instructors or authors must compensate for the ambient intellectual laziness by a commensurate flow of simplification and trivialization initiatives.

A most important locus where this intellectual laziness has been seen is in the world of essays. Even though the essay is a reigning form of learning in our modern world, and is still presented as a bold adventure in discovery, authors interested in complex issues are no longer able to count on readers being willing to hold up their part of the learning bargain and to spend the requisite effort to understand material that cannot always be easy to understand. So authors have to 'dumb down' and stylize complex issues in simplistic ways if they wish to be read.

This explains the growing popularity of blogs and other forms of intellectual 'burps,' and of the use of all sorts of ideological shorthand that economize on the costs of thinking. Bald opinions have replaced analysis, and the effort to blend different perspectives and synthesize them in a wholistic way has come to be regarded as unduly costly in terms of intellectual effort.

These ambient toxicities explain the sketchiness and the high degree of 'unfinishedness' that characterize a large number of policy files where serious critical probing has been lacking, and antiquated intellectual frameworks remain in good currency – for lack of a modicum of effort that would have been required to probe deeper into those files, and failure to exert the requisite critical thinking to understand why the intellectual frameworks in good currency should be discredited.

Unfinished business:
an attack on the pneumopathological

Over the years I have been regularly frustrated by colleagues', technocrats' and students' lack of interest in exploring the limitations of canonical paradigms in good currency, or by the strictures imposed by the mental prisons generated by the ideologies in vogue. Trying to get people to challenge their first impressions and to change their minds after going through some serious critical thinking is a battle zone.

Questioning the dominant *manière de voir* is perceived as too costly. The cost of thinking required to modify and to transform one's own perspective point has come to be regarded as unwarranted, whatever the inadequacy of the ruling apparatus or ideology.

As a result, in a large number of issue domains on the social, management and policy fronts, inadequate frames of reference still survive and cackle on due to the unwillingness of experts to indulge in any serious critical thinking, and to engage in new forms of inquiry.

This is particularly striking when dealing with wicked policy problems. Despite their importance, adequate approaches fail to emerge and be adopted to deal with such problems where goals are unclear or not agreed upon; where means-ends relationships are neither well established nor stable; and where the core issues are clearly not tractable with the old inquiring apparatus in use.

One of the major reasons for this reluctance is intellectual laziness. It would require investing significant intellectual resources to gain an appreciation of a new intellectual toolbox that is, perhaps, difficult to understand at first; to construct alternative approaches on the basis of unfamiliar assumptions; and to explore new perspectives defining new frontiers. In this sense, the 'policy and strategy sciences' (in the broadest sense) appear to have a tendency to stick to their zone of comfort, and to be criminally conservative – clinging to antiquarian frames of reference despite their relentless failures – unlike less crusty sciences that have not insisted on continuing to operate within a Newtonian world on the pretext that quantum mechanics was too difficult to understand!

This is an ever more debilitating tendency – the more complexity-and-uncertainty-tainted the issues are – compounding (1) inherent intellectual difficulties in learning new approaches; (2) the perils of engaging in argumentative skirmishes in an age of moral relativism where any opinion is regarded as equally valid as any other; and (3) the hyper-tolerance for claptrap, sophistry, and deceit in good currency by an intelligentsia entrapped by antiquarian frames of reference. This sort of context discourages any investment in new approaches. Indeed, anything that might disturb the intellectual comfort that the conventional views provide would appear to be unwelcome. Traditional disciplinary paradigms constitute ramparts against the development of heterodox perspectives that are automatically denounced as unscientific, amateurish, ill-founded in the disciplinary tradition, and/or frivolous (Toulmin 2001).

Yet there are moments when a curmudgeon feels the urge to have another kick at some of these difficult unfinished affairs before the annoyance fades away.

That is the motivation behind this book. Obviously, the list of issue domains that might qualify as being in need of revisiting with a refurbished frame of reference is so long that it might appear to be a hopelessly quixotic task. It is true that it would be naïve to attempt to right all the wrongs on this front, and that such a quest is bound to suffer from a certain degree of idiosyncrasy. Yet one has to start somewhere.

For the venture undertaken here, I have paid special attention to those problems: (1) which appear to have the highest degree of toxic negative general impact on public affairs; and (2) about which I know a little.

The central purpose of the exercise is to attack the *pneumopathological* – a word proposed by Eric Voegelin, and used recently by Robert Sibley to describe the state of "those who are morally insane, 'living' as it were, in a fantasy-world of self-righteousness" (Sibley 2013). Such a disordered consciousness is not only ascribable to intellectual laziness but to other dysfunctions as well, of which excessive politeness, political correctness, failure to confront, and unreasonable accommodation are not unimportant ones.

To attack the pneumopathological, a certain degree of methodological cruelty is necessary, in the way one deals with viruses. Yet it need not be done unceremoniously or sternly. Satire – "sarcasm, irony or wit used to expose abuses or folly"[3] – will be intended in all phases of our argumentation as a way to inject a scent of irreverence that may provoke the reader sufficiently to wake him up.

The general line of argument

My exploration will try to present three perspectives on the toxic impact of pneumopathology: how it undermines critical thinking and intellectual inquiry; how it generates toxic reductive perspectives (quantophrenia) and destructive blockages to collaborative governance (disloyalty); and how it would appear to blind observers to the real sources of the present Canadian *malaise* and block the road to imaginative repairs – except for those adventurous enough to launch inquiries *hors des sentiers battus*.

Part I deals frontally with two important impacts of the cognitive laziness that have prevailed over the last few decades in the world of public affairs: how the twilight of critical thinking has led to a dramatic weakening of the critical examination of issues; and how the process of inquiry has been significantly weakened by ever narrower perspectives and a consequent debilitation of the method of knowledge acquisition that has ensued.

Part II focuses on two mental prisons: the obsessive and reductive insistence on a quantophrenic twist (only that which can be quantified counts) that has dramatically dwarfed the

---

[3] www.merriam-webster.com/dictionary/satire.

ambit of the human sciences, their analyses, and their *force de frappe*; and the failure by crucial partners to live up to the requirements of their burden of office in circumstances which call for collaboration (in particular, at the political-bureaucratic interface) – a disloyalty that has considerably enfeebled the possibility of effective collaborative governance when it was imperative for organizations to succeed.

Part III injects a whiff of optimism in an argument that has been somewhat denunciatory in Parts I and II. It suggests that it is not impossible to break down the barriers to more synoptic approaches, and to more adventurous and imaginative organizational/institutional designs to deal with the challenges facing the Canadian socio-economy.

There are two steps to this: (1) by suggesting a synoptic diagnosis on the present Canadian *malaise* based on a synthetic approach; and (2) by showcasing most succinctly the work of Tom Courchene, a Canadian *savanturier* (a crasis of *savant* and *aventurier*), who has demonstrated throughout his career a particular capacity to reflect broadly on the pathologies of the Canadian socio-economy, and a particular boldness in proposing adventurous designs to repair our organizations and institutions. However, the fact that the right sort of work can be done, and that some social architects have done it, does not mean that it is either common practice, or that this work has received the attention it greatly deserves.

The conclusion makes the case for an approach that is both synoptic and guided by reasonableness – against the dogmas of disciplinary analyses and unduly skimpy rationality – and puts forward some reflections that may serve as guideposts in the sort of exploration that would appear to be called for … if any free-spirited *savanturier* is tempted to rise to the challenge.

Acknowledgements

Some of the issues discussed here have engaged me more or less actively at different times over the last several decades. At particular moments during this long period, alternative ripostes to these varied challenges have been developed, often in collaboration with colleagues and friends at the Centre on Governance over almost 20 years.

Some of these partners need to be explicitly acknowledged (Willem Gilles, Robin Higham, Ruth Hubbard and Christopher Wilson) but only to ensure that they not be regarded as guilty by association for the present account of our common ventures. Each of them should be held responsible only for the part of this heretical enterprise in which they have deliberately and actively participated – a matter clarified in the text. In no way should they shoulder any responsibility for the methodological cruelty displayed, or for any ill-tempered or unkind contents of this book. For this, I take full responsibility.

Many other colleagues, associated at one time or other with the *travails* of the Centre on Governance, have also been helpful partners in all sorts of ways. Although they may not all be explicitly identified below, they will all recognize, here and there in the text, echoes of discussions and forums in which they have actively and creatively participated. Their anonymous contribution is acknowledged.

Some earlier versions of a few chapters in this book have been published or presented to different audiences in slightly different forms. The details of these earlier versions have been recorded in a note on sources at the end of the book.

Finally, the material, financial and moral support of the Centre on Governance of the University of Ottawa over the years, and the editorial assistance of Anne Burgess are also gratefully acknowledged.

References

Brafman, Ori and Rod A. Beckstrom. 2006. *The Starfish and the Spider – The Unstoppable Power of Leaderless Organizations*. New York, NY: The Penguin Group.

Brown, Valerie A. 2008. *Leonardo's Vision – A guide to collective thinking and action*. Rotterdam, NL: Sense Publishers.

Hampden-Turner, Charles and Alfons Trompenaars. 1993. *The Seven Cultures of Capitalism*. New York, NY: Currency Doubleday.

Hubbard, Ruth and Gilles Paquet. 2014. *Probing the Bureaucratic Mind: About Canadian Federal Executives*. Ottawa, ON: Invenire Books.

Kahane, Adam. 2004. *Solving Tough Problems – An Open Way of Talking, Listening, and Creating New Realities*. San Francisco, CA: Berrett-Koehler Publishers.

Kleiner, Art. 2012. "The Thought Leader Interview of Dov Seidman." *Strategy & Business*, 67, Summer.

Michalko, Michael. 2012. "Cognitive Laziness Inhibits Creative Thinking," *The Creativity Post*, September 28.

Paquet, Gilles. 1999a. *Governance through Social Learning*. Ottawa, ON: University of Ottawa Press.

Paquet, Gilles. 1999b. "Tackling Wicked Problems" in G. Paquet. *Governance though Social Learning*. Ottawa, ON: University of Ottawa Press, p. 41-52.

Paquet, Gilles. 2009. *Scheming virtuously: The road to collaborative governance*. Ottawa, ON: Invenire Books, chapter 5.

Paquet, Gilles. 2013. *Tackling Wicked Policy Problems: Equality, Diversity, and Sustainability*. Ottawa, ON: Invenire Books, chapter 4.

Paquet, Gilles and Christopher Wilson. 2011. "Collaborative Co-governance as Inquiring Systems," *www.optimumonline.ca*, 41(2): 1-12.

Pynchon, Thomas R. 1961/1963. *V.* New York, NY: HarperCollins.

Rittel, Horst W.J. and Melvin M. Webber. 1973. "Dilemmas in a General Theory of Planning," *Policy Sciences* (4): 155-169.

Schön, Donald A. 1971. *Beyond the Stable State*. New York, NY: Norton.

Sibley, Robert. 2013. "Young men can be turned to good or evil," *The Ottawa Citizen*, April 29. http://www2.canada.com/ottawacitizen/news/archives/story.html?id=67b9004d-2cda-4c97-874b-fd8496e51ed6&p=2 [Accessed May 2, 2014].

Siegel, Jules. 1977. "Who Is Thomas Pynchon ... And Why Did He Take Off with My Wife?" *Playboy*, March.

Toulmin, Stephen. 2001. *Return to Reason*. Cambridge, MA: Harvard University Press.

PART I
On Liberating Learning

One of the important sources of intellectual blockages to social learning, to advances in our understanding of our world, and to the design of improved ways to better steward our organizations and institutions, has to do with learning disabilities. These disabilities are responsible for the failures in ensuring effective stewarding and wayfinding.

Not only are the learning disabilities costly in the short run, but they are even more costly in the longer run, since they entail a systematic misguiding of the process of continuous adjustment that is necessary to ensure the effective governance of organizations and institutions.

These foundational flaws will be probed in two steps.

First, the attention is focused on the impact of the demise of critical thinking. It has been responsible for the failure to develop a meaningful appreciative system capable of grappling with the growing complexity of modern organizations and institutions. This has undermined the whole process of description of the setting and circumstances of the issues of interest; thwarted the process of problem definition; and derailed the development of the multidimensional frameworks required to take into account the divergence of viewpoints, and to nudge into existence the requisite blending of perspectives capable of generating the appropriate trade-offs among the views of crucial partners to ensure commitment to collaborative governance and effective wayfinding.

Second, the focus is on the limitations of the whole process of inquiring and social learning in good currency, i.e., on the process of knowledge production necessary to fuel the continuous adjustment of organizations to the contextual change, and to the evolving changes in the needs and preferences of the different stakeholders that are in place. These prevent the emergence of the new modes of production of knowledge required to ensure the progress and survivability of organizations through the learning of new means, new ends, and the experimentation with new organizational designs calling for a modification of their very fabric and mission.

These blockages have distorted the way in which problems have been defined and approached, and have stunted social learning. In both cases, some initiatives have been proposed to correct the situation, but they have emerged with great slowness and clumsiness. Mindfulness having been undermined, and critical thinking having been stultified, the resilience and survivability of the organizations have been threatened. Some of the on-going transformations underway that promise a return of critical thinking and of more effective inquiring systems are hinted at. But it should be clear that dynamic conservatism is strong; nothing less than a revolution in the mind will be necessary.

| On Critical Thinking

"A curse on him who begins in gentleness.
He shall finish in insipidity and cowardice ..."
André Trocmé

Preamble

The concern that is at the origin of this paper emerged sharply on the occasion of a number of breakfast meetings, sponsored by the Association of Professional Executives of the Public Service of Canada (APEX). APEX provided a safe space where executives could engage in serious conversations about some of the difficult issues they were confronted with in their work. Over the 44 sessions of discussion between 2006 and 2009, it became apparent that there had been an erosion of critical thinking in the Canadian public service, as well as in other arenas in Canada over the last while (Hubbard and Paquet 2014).

The costs of this erosion of critical thinking, and of the ensuing danger that this capability might fall into disuse, were acknowledged. It was agreed that the issue needed to be discussed as a matter of priority, and that ways should be found to correct the situation.

The intent of this paper is to respond to that concern, and to reboot a taste for asking *why* and *how* – questions that powerfully expose sophistry and deceit, and that, by generating a modicum of anger in those whose arguments are exposed as bunk, leave them prone to reveal by their unpersuasive babblings the poverty of their arguments – but ultimately to make something different happen. This approach is akin to what is called in diplomatic circles the *French protocol* – a well-known strategy of French diplomats (I am told) to ensure, by appropriate techniques, that they make those defending views contrary to their own, feel more and more uncomfortable.

The argumentation proceeds in stages.

First, the tough problem of defining critical thinking is tackled. Second, a conceptual map is suggested – one that focuses on three flaws at the source of poor critical thinking, of which the lack of good critical description is one. Third, the crucial importance of mental prisons as a second blockage preventing critical thinking is underlined. Fourth, I focus on the insensitivity to the socio-ethical constraints in good currency as an additional blockage to effective critical thinking. Fifth, I propose a process of triangulation that holds the key to the refurbishment of critical thinking, and to a permanent regime of retooling, restructuring, reframing and social learning capable not only of fuelling effective critical thinking, but also of exploring new perspectives and ensuring that the difficulties posed by poor critical description, mental prisons and an impoverished appreciation of the socio-ethical constraints in place are overcome.

Defining critical thinking

> "Common sense is the most fairly distributed thing in the world, for each one thinks he is so well-endowed with it."
>
> *René Descartes*

Critical thinking is not a simple notion. When an international group of experts was asked to develop a consensus about the meaning of *critical thinking*, the result was not unlike the proverbial horse drawn up by a committee.[1]

Less verbose, but not less daunting, is the definition of *what critical thinkers do* – raise vital questions; formulate them clearly; gather relevant information and interpret it effectively; come to well-reasoned conclusions and decisions; test them on relevant criteria; think open-mindedly about alternative perspectives, assessing as needed their assumptions and consequences; and communicate effectively with others in figuring out solutions.

More succinctly, one might choose Schafersman's definition of critical thinking as "reasonable, reflective, responsible, and skillful thinking that is focused on deciding what to believe or do" (Schafersman 1991: 3).

More analytically, one may prefer the definition proposed by Gabennesch (2006) that focuses on the three broad prerequisites for critical thinking – *thinking skills* (analyzing, synthesizing, interpreting, explaining, evaluating, generalizing, abstracting, illustrating, applying, comparing, recognizing logical fallacies), a *skeptic's worldview* (things are not always entirely what they seem as the first wisdom of critical thinking), and a commitment to *intellectual due process*

---

[1] "We understand critical thinking to be purposeful, self-regulatory judgment which results in interpretation, analysis, evaluation, and inference, as well as explanation of the evidential, conceptual, methodological, criteriological, or contextual considerations upon which that judgment is based. CT is essential as a tool of inquiry. As such, CT is a liberating force in education and a powerful resource in one's personal and civic life. While not synonymous with good thinking, CT is a pervasive and self-rectifying human phenomenon. The ideal critical thinker is habitually inquisitive, well-informed, trustful of reason, open-minded, flexible, fair-minded in evaluation, honest in facing personal biases, prudent in making judgments, willing to reconsider, clear about issues, orderly in complex matters, diligent in seeking relevant information, reasonable in the selection of criteria, focused in inquiry, and persistent in seeking results which are as precise as the subject and the circumstances of inquiry permit. Thus, educating good critical thinkers means working toward this ideal. It combines developing CT skills with nurturing those dispositions which consistently yield useful insights and which are the basis of a rational and democratic society" (Quoted in Facione 2009).

(more integrity, humility, tolerance of uncertainty, and raw courage than most of us find easy to summon).

Whatever the definition used, critical thinking is not something that everyone practices, or anything that everyone is good at all the time. Most agents do not have the combination of skills, worldview and vigilance required to meet these sorts of standards of coherence, self-awareness, honesty, open-mindedness and mindfulness.

Moreover, most agents also do not realize that critical thinking must address issues in two steps: reducing harms (eliminating the blockages preventing the inquiry to proceed effectively), and then exploring this decontaminated terrain in order to uncover preferable alternative ways both to proceed with the inquiry, and to imagine and develop better approaches and arrangements likely to ensure better coordination. While on the surface, working at reducing bad things may look the same as promoting good things, they are not. At the operational level, it makes a considerable difference, and entails substantially different ways of thinking: "scrutinizing the harms themselves, and discovering their dynamics and dependencies, leads to the possibility of sabotage. Cleverly conceived acts of sabotage, exploiting identified vulnerabilities of the object under attack, can be not only effective, but extremely resource-efficient too" (Sparrow 2008: 27). Without such decontamination and clearing of the ground, it is often impossible and always difficult to undertake the design of preferable governance arrangements through retooling, restructuring, and reframing.

Even under the most auspicious circumstances (and in the company of the best intentioned partners), critical thinking is quite a daunting task. The very daunting nature of the task often triggers *counter-adaptive preferences*. Since the task is so challenging, persons are likely to label it as being ill-inspired, uncivil, unnecessary, and even toxic – and therefore unwanted. This is the well-known *sour grapes phenomenon* (Elster 1983; Paquet 2013: chapter 2). Less generous labels for such attitudes might be cognitive dissonance, denial, willful blindness, weakness of will, failure to confront and political correctness (Higham and Paquet 2013). And the persiflage perpetrated by those who are unwilling to be critical thinkers turns out to be little more than rationalizations for rolling over, escapism and intellectual irresponsibility.

Critical description for critical thinking

"It isn't what we don't know that gives us trouble,
it's what we know that ain't so."

Will Rogers

Critical thinking is a *manière de voir*, a commitment not to put up with bullshit (Frankfurt 1988, 2005), an engagement to ask always and systematically why and how, and a commitment to insist on maintaining persistent relentless vigilance continually and in all circumstances.

This vigilant propensity to enhance the *integrity of the process of inquiry* itself requires *thinking skills, a skeptic's worldview,* and *intellectual due process* in a manner that is as free of failures and slippages as possible. However, this is too general a way of stating what has to be done. A more specific way to proceed is to recognize that the flaws at the source of poor critical thinking might be regarded as resulting from three major blockages: *poor critical description* of the context and the organization; *mental prisons* preventing as extensive an examination of the issues as possible; and poor appreciation of the *socio-ethical constraints* in good currency in a particular social system.

These three blockages are dealt with sequentially in this and the following sections.

John Dewey used to say "in the beginning is the issue." This calls for an appreciation of the complexity of the situation one is facing, and depends on a mastery of the art of critical description. Description is the poor sister of prediction and prescription in the methodology literature, but predictive and prescriptive analyses are dependent on effective description to start with.

To gain a meaningful appreciation of any context requires much practice. The illumination provided by critical description depends on the accumulated stock of knowledge, but also on a capacity for a discriminating understanding that comes with exposure to a multiplicity of cases, commingling all the intertwined economic, political and social forces at play. Usually, this knowledge of context and an appreciation of the complexity of the issues are the result of experience in a sector or field. Extensive experience refines the capacity for critical description and improves the ability to define complex issues well (Gladwell 2005). This is what we mean when we say that a person has a good appreciation of the 'world of business,' or the 'world of medicine.'

Checklists may help to avoid mishaps in describing. A checklist is nothing more than a *pense-bête*: a sort of reminder that one should be mindful of certain important things to check to begin with, and along the way, in order to avoid disaster. It is used by pilots in cockpits before taking off, by surgeons in operating rooms, by rock climbers, etc. with immense benefits (Gawande 2009).

A checklist for critical description is always *provisional,* and *bound to evolve with experience and social learning.* As such, it does not make a wise intellectual rock-climber; it is only a reminder of a number of checks that might help the intellectual rock climber to avoid a bad fall.

For example, are there:
- any explicit or implicit assumptions being made about the setting or the operations of the organization of interest and its governance that need to be questioned?
- any mechanisms that are presumed to be at work, and do we know under what conditions and circumstances such mechanisms will or will not operate well?
- safeguards in place to prevent faulty reasoning from going unchallenged? Are the necessary principles of mindfulness necessary to ensure a capacity to react quickly to the unexpected well-anchored in organizational arrangements (attention to anomalies,

preoccupation with failure, reluctance to simplify, sensitivity to operations, commitment to resilience, deference to expertise)?

• blockages in the process of social learning that might obscure, delay, or prevent the necessary retooling, restructuring, reframing or re-founding of the organization from proceeding as a result of social learning?

There is nothing comprehensive or definitive about this evolving checklist, but it ensures that certain important points are kept in mind and discussed in the face of present *malaises*.

Exorcizing mental prisons to avoid crippling epistemologies

> "What has once been thought cannot be unthought."
>
> *Friedrich Dürrenmatt*

The checklist can go some way toward improving mindfulness. But it cannot do much about the willful blindness and distorting ideologies that play a significant role in crippling epistemologies (Paquet 2009a).

It is necessary to be mindful of the *intellectual baggage* that the agent brings with him/her in the process of inquiry, which can distort the perceptions and derail the argument. This is the second major blockage to critical thinking.

There are a number of mental prisons linked to identity that serve as stoppers of critical thinking: commitment to disciplines as reductive lenses, to dogmas based on systems of beliefs, to norms that command a suspension of judgment – like hyper-tolerance, collegiality, political correctness, obsessive risk aversion, etc. Such *servitudes* need not be just the submission to the dominant view of one person or group of opinion molders. It may well be submissiveness to an idea, a canonical text, or a point of view, that selectively focuses only on certain aspects of the context, and considers the rest as irrelevant and of no import.

These mental prisons create a filtre, and trigger a form of self-censorship that restricts considerably the realm of what is regarded as relevant knowledge to be explored, and the evaluation of its worth. This sort of censorship brings forth a mode of acquisition of knowledge that is fundamentally flawed, because it is dramatically reductive and/or distorted, and suggests ways of handling governance challenges that often are wrong-headed because of the truncated view of the world that has inspired them.

In many cases, the particular canonical view of the world in good currency may be such that members are likely to react as if they had been indoctrinated in a cult and be led to unwittingly make *assumptions they are not even aware they are making*. This leads to the damning of those who do not share the canonical view as simply uttering sheer nonsense, being feeble-minded, or revealing moral failure. In such cases, the capacity for reflexive examination of one's own assumptions and of one's actions is stunted.

Nobody is free from ideological bents, or from assumptions they are not aware they are making. Claiming to be free of such mental prisons is a sign of either great naïvety or of duplicity. And exorcizing such biases is quite difficult because they are intertwined with identity and group belonging.

Such mental prisons may be personal or organizational. One may be trapped by one's own system of personal beliefs. But the milieu may also be the source of the mental prison. An organization may be more or less permissive, may more or less encourage delinquency, may tolerate or prohibit more or less aggressive use of moral imagination to exploit terrains at the borders of the corridor of acceptable behaviour, etc. This sort of organizational iron cage may appear somewhat difficult to grapple with, but it can be decoded in an oblique way by unveiling the sort of characteristics, fantasies and dangers that an organizational culture might encourage or discourage, with the result that, in order to survive, individuals are led inexorably either to adopt the view in good currency, or to leave the organization altogether.

In no organization can it be said that all assumptions are allowed to be questioned, and all members can allow themselves to tinker with mechanisms, structures and norms in use. Indeed, it is generally the other way around. Most organizations have an 'appreciative system' and those who do not share it are regarded as deviants, outsiders.

Indeed, most institutions are more or less *neurotic* (Kets de Vries and Miller 1984; Kets de Vries 2001). Kets de Vries and Miller have proposed a typology of neurotic styles plaguing organizations (the characteristics, fantasies, culture and dangers attached to these different styles, and considerably limiting the possibility of critical thinking). They are spelled out in the following table.

A cursory reading of the table will convey a sense of what each sort of iron cage may entail for those operating within such types of organizations. In each case, when a dominant neurotic style or another prevails, the crippling impact and the challenges are different, and different ways have to be designed for the neurotic style to be effectively attenuated.

A most useful exercise for the reader would be to look at his/her own organization through the lens of the Kets de Vries-Miller perspective. The central questions would be: which of the neuroses would appear to fit my organization best; and what could be done to attenuate the distorting effects of this neurosis? [2]

[2] These ideal-types are vignettes that are not necessarily meant to represent realistic pictures of organizations. At best it indicates a prevalent syndrome in a world where real organizations are often a mix of types. I had an experience with this sort of exercise in May 1990, at a management conference held by Statistics Canada at Mont Ste. Marie, Quebec. I used this template to show that Statistics Canada corresponded to the ideal-type for compulsive organizations. This generated much chagrin at the executive level but an extraordinarily animated discussion in the broader group, to the point that the event is still mentioned 20 years later. One lesson is that the instrument should be used with care (Paquet 1990). Kets de Vries (2001) has designed

The clinical intervention necessary to unlock the mental prisons, and to succeed in making sure the bias is attenuated (or at the very least recognized if not fully exorcized), is often very challenging and not easily performed.

Some success in getting both the personal and the organizational mental prisons factored into the discussion would at the very least allow some dialogue about the existence of the biases, and foster the emergence of ways to keep them in check (Yankelovich 1999).[3]

---

a simple questionnaire to determine to what neurotic style one's own organization would appear to belong, and to what extent any one person may be said to fit well within it. In many exercises with such a questionnaire, in executive development seminars, a variety of diagnoses about the same organization emerged depending on the points of view of the different actors about the nature of the neurosis, but most often there was a great deal of convergence of diagnoses.

[3] An interesting macro-system experiment with dialogue has been generated by the work of the General Agreement on Tariffs and Trade (GATT) – an international organization with minimal executive power that was called the General Agreement on Talking and Talking by economists. In a few decades of international dialogue, the tariff barriers were dramatically slashed among most countries of the planet.

SUMMARY OF THE NEUROTIC STYLES

	Paranoid (suspicious)	Compulsive	Dramatic	Depressive	Schizoid (detached)
Characteristics	mistrust much info processing hypersensitivity perceived threats centralized power	perfectionism rigid formal code focus on trivia ritualized evaluation dogmatism	self-dramatization overcentralized narcissism 2nd-tier lacking influence exploitativeness	sense of guilt ritualism helplessness unflexibility bureaucracy	non-involvement internal focus estrangement self-imposed barriers to information insufficient scanning of environment
Fantasy	I cannot really trust anybody; I had better be on my guard	I don't want to be at the mercy of events; I must control all things	I want to get attention from and impress people	It is hopeless to change the course of events in my offer; I am not good enough	The world of reality does not offer any satisfaction so it is safer to remain distant
Culture	fear of attack intimidation uniformity reactive conservative secretive	rigidity inward directed tightly focused obsessive non-adaptive exhaustive evaluation	idealizing hyperactive impulsive bold ventures non participative action for action's sake	lacking initiative decidophobia lacking vigilance leadership vacuum no sense of direction lacking motivation	insecurity conflict ridden indecisive inconsistent narrow perspectives lacking warmth
Dangers	distorsion of reality defensive attitude	fear of making mistakes excessive reliance on rules	overreaction to minor events actions based on appearances	inhibition of action indecisiveness overly pessimistic	bewilderment and aggressiveness emotional isolation

Source: Adapted from Kets de Vries & Miller (1984), p. 24-25 and Kets de Vries (2001), p. 146-147.

Preventing asocial and unethical conduct and outcomes

"... we have simply developed bad habits ..."
Dietrich Dörner

Critical thinking does not pertain only to matters of logic and coherence, or to epistemological failures ascribable to mental prisons upstream. There is also an immense potential for failures downstream – when lack of critical thinking leads to actions that would appear to fall outside the corridor of the acceptable in either the organization or the environment.

Governing has become an ongoing conversation within and among the various *games without a master* that colligate agents and groups in various ways when power, resources and information of all sorts are widely distributed. The new basic unit of analysis in this maelstrom is *the relation*. These relations can be defined as types of *contractual relations* (economic, social, political, cultural, moral, etc.) that can be embodied in more or less formal terms. In any relationship, such a 'contract' attempts to roughly define what would match the legitimate expectations of the partners, and constitute the foundations of both accountability (what is the *expected* performance) and ethics (what is regarded as *acceptable* performance) (Paquet 1991, 1997; Lecours and Paquet 2006).

In order to develop the sort of apparatus likely to generate effective wayfinding in such a world, one must be able to build (1) not only on a good *appreciation of context*; and (2) a sense of the *extent to which the different organizations allow more or less latitude* in the redefining and the re-framing of issues according to circumstances and what has been learned along the way; but also, (3) on the broad set of *reference points* that define 'good' behaviour for the different stakeholders – both in terms of the sociality in vogue (social norms in good currency) and in terms of the prevailing hyper-sociality (ethical and moral norms underpinning the social rules).

That is the position of Margaret Somerville (2000), who defines her minimalist *ethical canary* as based on two focal points: respect for life and protecting the human spirit.

Another minimalist benchmark that might serve as a reference is the balancing of the imperatives of the four cardinal virtues: (i) *temperantia* – an awareness and sense of limits; (ii) *fortitudo* – a capacity to take into account context and the long term; (iii) *justitia* – a sense of what is good, and an inclination to search for it; and (iv) *prudentia* – a sense of what is practical and reasonable.

This entails a mindfulness about not only a good appreciation of the *context* and of the *organizational culture*, but also an appreciation of both (1) the *sociality* (i.e., the constraints and the degrees of freedom that the society's *common public culture* avails its members in developing strategies within a certain corridor; and the support or non-support for any effort by agents to extend the width of the corridor of acceptable behaviour by society); and (2) the sort of basic references to *hyper-sociality* or focal points by reference to which acceptable behaviour might be defined in ethical terms. These references determine where the lines in the sand are, the boundaries one can and should not cross, and the zones of moral comfort and discomfort (Heath 2003; Caldwell 2012).

Triangulation I: to undo harms

> *"Penser, c'est dire non ..."*
> *Alain*

It is in the triangulation of these different dimensions (context, organizational culture and sociality, and hyper-sociality) that one has to find ways to navigate safely: safety amounting to ensuring that decisions and designs are developed in a manner that honours all moral contracts, and that can be explained in a language that all would find acceptable.

Whatever the constraints imposed by poor critical description, flawed organizational culture and sociality, and the violation of the foundational values used as anchors, critical thinking and learning entail a protocol of triangulation among these three sets of constraints in an effort to understand the situation, to decontaminate it, and to design the sort of wayfinding likely to yield value adding, resilience and progress for the organization.

None of these elements is rock solid. The critical appreciation of the context is always somewhat imperfect; the organizational culture and sociality are more or less fully and accurately gauged and are always evolving; the reference values or hyper-sociality are always more or less debatable, and are also evolving. Moreover, issues migrate among levels: in certain countries or in certain organizations, what was once an ethical issue may have become so ingrained in the sociality that one might speak of it having become a cultural issue – a cultural given.

This triangulation process of social learning (based on a continuous *negotiation* among agents to ascertain the boundaries of the corridor of acceptable performance) cannot be operationalized without an appreciation of the evolving context. This, in turn, calls for some continuous reconstruction and re-interpretation. Ultimately, it is a process based on a need for imagination (social and moral) *to extend the corridor of acceptable performance* by developing new prototypes or extending existing ones. Triangulation work develops a sort of *cumulative connoisseurship* that over time should produce reflexes that generate responses "in a blink" (Paquet 1997).

To know whether one is at the boundary of the corridor or out of bounds, one may have to count on some level of discomfort (some discomfort index) or some sensitivities being developed over time by exposition to a great variety of circumstances. This leads to adjustments that are not only the result of deliberations. They are often the result of demographic reshuffling of the deck of actors, or of the mechanical mechanisms of thresholds and cascading effects (Granovetter 1978).

Such correctives to undo or attenuate harm often emerge (like the orange wave in the last federal election, or the student protest in Quebec in the spring of 2012) as a result of a contagion much more than mere deliberation (Paquet 2012a).

In the introduction to an English translation of the play *Rhinocéros* by Eugène Ionesco, Denis de Rougemont recalls how the idea for the play emerged. The play is about characters being transformed suddenly into rhinoceroses. De Rougemont recalls that he and Ionesco were by chance witnessing a Nazi parade in Germany in the 1930s when they found themselves caught up in the frenzy of the crowd, and instinctively making the 'Heil Hitler' salute. It forcefully illustrates the power of a contagion.

The process of triangulation is *part deliberation, part exploration and probing, part learning by doing and experimenting* with organizational design and moral imagination to reconcile the multiplicity of moral contracts, *part as a result of redefining the boundaries* of the 'social and moral corridors' defining the locus of what is and is not acceptable (Paquet 2002, 2005a, 2005b), and *part movements of contagion.* This is quite a messy evolution, full of fits and starts that lead nowhere, and of small initiatives at tipping points triggering important changes.

The cumulative requirements that have been garnered to ensure effective critical thinking at the beginning of this paper explain why the task of fending off and attenuating harms is so daunting. All sorts of requirements were mentioned:

- thinking skills, a skeptic's worldview, intellectual due process;
- a checklist to ensure the integrity of the process of inquiry;
- an appreciation of the mental prisons, assumptions people are not aware they are making, etc., brought by partners into the conversation;
- a fair awareness of the latitude afforded by the sociality or organizational culture for partners to engage in retooling, restructuring, and reframing in the different contexts;
- a distillation of the hyper-sociality or ethical boundaries defining not only what is technically feasible, but also what is socially acceptable and morally permissible in a given social context; and finally,
- the sort of acceptable rules in the conduct of the triangulation process bringing all those dimensions

into some sort of balance in the process of wayfinding, experimenting, exploring, social learning and innovating. The sort of intellectual power, skills and mindfulness required to conduct critical thinking is such that it is hardly surprising that it has been found taxing, and that humans have found refuge in systems of belief that economize greatly on critical thinking by copious reliance on dogma, articles of faith, encompassing ideologies, disciplinary codes, and the like – with an etiquette of hyper-tolerance, political correctness, and failure to confront to ensure that conversations are appropriately sanitized.

Yet critical thinking as mainly a defensive *conformance* tool – to undo or to prevent failures and harms – cannot suffice. Critical thinking must also be a creative tool. It must fuel the design process and generate the emergence of new forms of organizational arrangements capable of thrusting the organization in new innovative directions, i.e., triangulation is meant not only to reveal the limits of the existing apparatus, but also and mainly to serve as a platform from which one can explore and design alternative ways, and promise innovation and better performance.

Triangulation II: to design new alternatives

"L'humanité ne doit qu'à l'insolence d'avoir grandi et prospéré ..."
Jean Michel Besnier

Critical thinking is an activity also meant to underpin and fuel the experimentation with prototypes in view of designing alternative systems that do not yet exist (Perlmutter 1965; Romme 2003). This calls for a new frame of mind which leads to approaching organizations with a *design attitude*. It has already begun in the world of business (Martin 2009), but it has been much slower on other fronts.

This new way of thinking requires from practitioners a *modicum of irreverence* (in order to be able to escape from the mental prisons in good currency, or disciplinary codes, or loosely theorized dogmas) and a *certain amount of audacity and courage* (to engage in more risky ventures – *la marine en long*, exploring the high seas in search of new continents) is fundamentally different from the secure *marine en large* that is satisfied to engage in the intellectual equivalent of routine ferry-boating such as between Cumberland (Ontario) and Gatineau (Quebec) on the Ottawa river.

This irreverence will require finding the fortitude to attack and subvert some articles of faith in the scripture of theories of decision making in good currency. Three conspicuous ideas have to be challenged: (1) *the pre-existence of purpose* (be they labeled needs, values, preferences, wants, goals, etc.) when purpose is learned along the way; (2) *the necessity of consistency* that may at times prohibit the very initiative likely to trigger adjustment; and (3) the *primacy of instrumental rationality* (March 1988: chapter 12).

March has five suggestions as a small beginning in this task:
- *treat goals as hypotheses;*
- *treat intuition as real* (i.e., take seriously anything that seems to be outside the present scheme for justifying behaviour);
- *treat hypocrisy as a transition* (i.e., do not treat inconsistency as a vice and do not allow it to prevent experimentation);
- *treat memory as an enemy* (i.e., consider the possibility that memory prevents experimentation that may well pay off); and
- *treat experience as a theory* (i.e., allowing experience to have a conceptual status and to drive our thinking as much as frozen conclusions from the past).

As March would put it, all these procedures represent "a way in which we temporarily suspend the operation of the system of reasoned intelligence. They are playful" (*Ibid.*: 263).

But irreverence is not sufficient.

Design also requires a modicum of audacity: it cannot be reduced to problem-solving steps, fully programmable under a set of rules (Schön 1990). This is unduly reductive, since it assumes that the problem space (like an actual maze) has a structure that is already given. The design process does not really start with such givens. Schön defines it as the *intelligent exploration of a terrain* (*Ibid.*: 125), as an inquiry guided by an appreciative system, carried over from history and past experience, that produces "a selective representation of an unfamiliar situation that sets values for the system's transformation. It frames the problem of the problematic situation, and thereby sets directions in which solutions lie, and provides a schema for exploring them" (*Ibid.*: 131-2).

Designing is a conversation with the situation that leads to experimenting with rules and guideposts. That sort of exercise reveals conflicts and dilemmas in the appreciative system. Since participants talk across discrepant frames, designing "is a process in which communication, political struggle, and substantive inquiry are combined … [and it] may be judged appropriate … if it leads to the creation of a design structure that directs inquiry toward progressively greater inclusion of features of the problematic situation and values for its transformation" (*Ibid.*: 138-9).

Such exploration leads to learning by doing, and "involves inquiry into systems that do not yet exist" (Romme 2003: 558). It requires a heightened attention to organizational design and to the theory and practice of social architecture (Perlmutter 1965). This, in turn, requires *design thinking*: (1) a way of thinking that escapes *groupthink and convergent thinking designed to **make** choices* – and favours *divergent thinking designed to **create** choice possibilities*; (2) a shift from the *exploitation* of existing knowledge to *exploration* for new knowledge; and (3): *a shift from routine management to the continuous reinvention of the organization, from short term and low risk to long term and high risk undertakings* (Schumacher 1977; March 1991).

This new way of thinking builds on experimentation, prototyping, and serious play (Schrage 2000: 199ff; Paquet 2009a: 8), and makes the highest and best use of grappling, grasping, discerning and sense-making as part of reflective generative learning. It bypasses the simple use of focus groups, public engagement exercises, and surveys as rearview mirrors into the future, because, as Tim Brown reminds us, Henry Ford used to say – "if I'd asked my customers what they wanted, they'd have said a faster horse." Design thinking is a systematic approach to innovation: not being satisfied with managing existing offerings and adapting them to new users, but creating new offerings for new users (Brown 2009: 40, 261; Hubbard and Paquet 2013).

This *new spirit* approaches description, mental prisons and ethical constraints quite differently: (1) it engages in *re-description as a result of a new manière de voir*; (2) it uses *lateral thinking* and the reframing of perspectives; (3) it identifies and *relaxes all assumptions* and unfreezes the organizational culture to increase as much as possible the latitude the organization grants for exploration outside the box (De Bono 1967; Paquet 2009a); and (4) it makes *maximum use of moral imagination* to redefine the ethical constraints and make them not only more malleable but more useable to scheme virtuously (Johnson 1993; Paquet 2009b).

Conclusion

One cannot presume that a taste for *critical thinking* can be regenerated overnight after a long period when it has been systematically discouraged, and has gone into hibernation. It would be equally naïve to believe that a *design attitude* will emerge instantaneously.

Critical thinking is fundamentally a matter of learning by doing, of what has come to be known as *professional wrighting and wroughting* (Paquet 2009a: chapter 2). It is practical knowledge rooted in *savoir-faire (delta knowledge)*, and is different from the usual types of knowledge developed in the humanities, experimental sciences and social sciences (Paquet 2012b). Such a *manière de voir*, and the attitude that best accompanies it, will need to be nurtured.

Ground zero is *mindfulness* that fosters learning. That point has already been made.

Phase I is a greater awareness of the cost of the erosion of critical thinking. Again, this was broached earlier, but more needs to be said to persuade sleepwalking observers before they can come out of their catatonia. As Higham and Paquet (2013) have shown – and as it will be discussed in chapter 5 – the lack of critical thinking has already led to a sanitization of language, a refusal to confront even the worst sophistry and deception, and a sheepish acceptance of even the most unreasonable accommodation in the name of tolerance – which is often a code name for the expiation for imaginary sins (Gottfried 2002). This, as Justice Sopinka (1992) wrote, is in danger of becoming the most important impediment to free speech.

Phase II is both the recognition that there are reasons to be concerned about these developments, and that their causes and sources need to be probed. This, in turn, calls for the highest and best use of irony and irreverence to challenge the assemblage of disingenuity, sophistry and bullshit that is currently posturing as conventional wisdom in academe and elsewhere, and is the result of the demise of critical thinking. Nothing less than methodological and intellectual cruelty is required. How else can one hope to awaken those who only pretend to sleep?

Phase III is the behavioural change that will reinstate the former natural proclivity of humans to ask *why* and *how* as a matter of course. A gentle first step might be a campaign to encourage the questioning of all assumptions. But this will not suffice. What must be mustered is the courage and audacity to declare an open season for the slaughtering of sacred cows: humanely, but relentlessly and mercilessly … one at a time … every day.

These sacred cows are crowding everywhere. This is not a new phenomenon: the very presence of these false idols and of their institutional entrapments – now as in the time of Francis Bacon (1620) or E.H. Gombrich (1979) – are the source of the corruption of the human sciences. Not being actively involved in the slaughtering is being complicit with the obscurantism the sacred cows generate, and contributing to the indefinite postponement of more mature human sciences focused on exploration and design.

But before proceeding, it is crucial to improve our mode of inquiring.

References

Bacon, Francis. 1620. *Novum Organum Scientiarum*. http://en.wikipedia.org/wiki/Novum_Organum [Accessed April 22, 2014].

Bennis, Warren. 1976. *The Unconscious Conspiracy*. New York, NY: AMACOM.

Brown, Tim. 2009. *Change by Design*. New York, NY: Harper Business.

Caldwell, Gary. 2012. *Canadian Public Culture*. Ste-Edwidge-de-Clifton, QC: The Fermentation Press.

De Bono, Edward. 1967. *The Use of Lateral Thinking*. London, UK: Jonathon Cape.

Dewey, John. 1935. *Liberalism and Social Action*. New York, NY: Putnam.

Elster, Jon. 1983. *Sour Grapes*. Cambridge, UK: Cambridge University Press.

Facione, P.A. 2009. *Critical Thinking: What it is and why it counts*. www.insightassessment.com [Accessed April 22, 2014].

Frankfurt, Harry G. 1988. *The importance of what we care about*. Cambridge, UK: Cambridge University Press.

Frankfurt, Harry G. 2005. *On Bullshit*. Princeton, NJ: Princeton University Press.

Gabennesch, H. 2006. "Critical Thinking ... What is it good for? (In fact, what is it?)," *Skeptical Inquirer*, 30(2): 36-41.

Gawande, Atul. 2009. *The Checklist Manifesto – How to get things right*. New York, NY: Metropolitan Books.

Gilles, Willem and Gilles Paquet. 1989. "On Delta Knowledge" in Gilles Paquet and Max von Zür Muehlen (eds.). *Edging toward the Year 2000*. Ottawa, ON: Canadian Federation of Deans of Management and Administrative Studies, p. 15-30.

Gladwell, Malcolm. 2005. *Blink: The Power of Thinking without Thinking*. New York, NY: Little Brown.

Gombrich, E.H. 1979. *Ideals and Idols*. New York, NY: Phaidon.

Gottfried, Paul Edward. 2002. *Multiculturalism and the Politics of Guilt*. Columbia, MO: University of Missouri Press.

Granovetter, Mark. 1978. "Threshold Models of Collective Behavior," *American Journal of Sociology*, 83(6): 1420-1443.

Heath, Joseph. 2003. *The Myth of Shared Values in Canada*. Ottawa, ON: Canadian Centre for Management Development.

Higham, Robin and Gilles Paquet. 2013. "Reflections on the Canadian Malaise," *www.optimumonline.ca*, 43(2): 1-13.

Hubbard, Ruth and Gilles Paquet 2010. *The Black Hole of Public Administration*. Ottawa, ON: University of Ottawa Press.

Hubbard, Ruth and Gilles Paquet. 2013. "Innovation as Redesign," *www.optimumonline.ca*, 43(4): 1-13.

Hubbard, Ruth and Gilles Paquet. 2014. *Probing the Bureaucratic Mind : About Canadian Federal Executives*. Ottawa, ON: Invenire Books.

Johnson, Mark. 1993. *Moral Imagination: Implications of Cognitive Science for Ethics*. Chicago, IL: University of Chicago Press.

Kets de Vries, Manfred F.R. 2001. *The Leadership Mystique*. London/New York: Financial Times/Prentice Hall.

Kets de Vries, Manfred F.R. and Dan Miller. 1984. *The Neurotic Organization*. San Francisco, CA: Jossey-Bass Publishers.

Lecours, Pierre and Gilles Paquet. 2006. "Communication and Ethics: How to Scheme Virtuously," *www.optimumonline.ca*, 36(2): 12-26.

March, James G. 1988. "The Technology of Foolishness" in J.G. March. *Organizations and Decisions*. Oxford, UK: Basil Blackwell.

March, James G. 1991. "Exploration and Exploitation in Organizational Learning," *Organization Science*, 2, p. 71-87.

Martin, Roger. 2009. *The Design of Business*. Boston, MA: Harvard Business Press.

Paquet, Gilles. 1990. "*The Statistical Agency as Janus.*" Mimeo, 8p.

Paquet, Gilles. 1991. "Betting on Moral Contracts," *Optimum,* 22(3): 45-53.

Paquet, Gilles. 1997. "The Burden of Office, Ethics and Connoisseurship," *Canadian Public Administration,* 40(1): 45-71.

Paquet, Gilles. 2002. "L'éthique est un sagesse toujours en chantier. Réflexions sur l'éthique et la gouvernance," *Ethique publique,* 4(1) : 62-76.

Paquet, Gilles. 2005a. *Gouvernance : une invitation à la subversion.* Montreal, QC: Liber.

Paquet, Gilles. 2005b. "L'éthique organisationnelle : pour un bricolage reconstructeur" in L. Langlois et. al. (eds.). *Ethique et dilemmes dans les organisations.* Quebec, QC: Laval University Press, p. 149-165.

Paquet, Gilles. 2009a. *Crippling Epistemologies and Governance Failures – A Plea for Experimentalism.* Ottawa, ON: University of Ottawa Press.

Paquet, Gilles. 2009b. *Scheming virtuously: The road to collaborative governance.* Ottawa, ON: Invenire Books.

Paquet, Gilles. 2012a. "Deux hoquets de gouvernance: affaire Montfort et grogne étudiante québécoise en 2012," *www. optimumonline.ca,* 42(2): 32-60.

Paquet, Gilles. 2012b. "La gouvernance, science de l'imprécis," *Organisations & Territoires,* 21(3): 5-17.

Paquet, Gilles. 2013. *Tackling Wicked Policy Problems: Equality, Diversity and Sustainability.* Ottawa, ON: Invenire Books.

Perlmutter, Howard V. 1965. *Towards a Theory and Practice of Social Architecture – The Building of Indispensable Institutions.* London, UK: Tavistock Publications.

Romme, A. George L. 2003. "Making a Difference: Organization as Design," *Organization Science,* 14(5): 558-573.

Schafersman, S.D. 1991. *An Introduction to Critical Thinking*. http://facultycenter.ischool.syr.edu/wp-content/uploads/2012/02/Critical-Thinking.pdf [Accessed May 25, 2014].

Schön, Donald A. 1971. *Beyond the Stable State*. New York, NY: Norton.

Schön, Donald A. 1990. "The Design Process" in V.A Howard (ed.). *Varieties of Thinking*. New York, NY: Routledge, p. 110-141.

Schrage, Michael. 2000. *Serious Play*. Boston, MA: Harvard Business School Press.

Schumacher, E. Fritz. 1977. *A Guide for the Perplexed*. New York, NY: Harper & Row.

Somerville, Margaret. 2000. *The Ethical Canary*. Toronto, ON: Viking.

Sopinka, John. 1992. "Freedom of Speech under Attack" in M.R. Byers (ed.). *The Empire Club of Canada Speeches 1991-1992*. Toronto, ON: The Empire Club Foundation, p. 508-522.

Sparrow, Malcolm K. 2008. *The Character of Harms*. Cambridge, UK: Cambridge University Press.

Yankelovich, Daniel. 1999. *The Magic of Dialogue – Transforming Conflict into Cooperation*. New York, NY: Simon & Schuster.

CHAPTER 2[1]

| On Inquiring

"Re-framing ... like an unexpected move on a chessboard can give the whole situation a new look ..."
Charles Handy

Introduction

The stylized version of strategy and policy actions in good currency in the post-World War II period (inherited from the surge of operations research during the war) was based on the assumptions: (1) that problems are well-structured *ab ovo*, and the goals known and agreed to by all, and (2) that the challenge is simply to design control

---

[1] This chapter is based on work originating in the 1970s to question the bow-arrow-target operations research model of strategy and policy based on mechanistic and reductive views in terms of goals and control mechanisms to reach them. This mechanistic approach was the dominant framework. Then the alternative proposed at the time (Paquet 1971) was based on the process of exploration of the feasible, starting with a tentative initial formulation, and strong feedback mechanisms fuelling social learning through transduction. This apparatus was further refined in the 1980s (Paquet 1989a; Gilles, W. and G. Paquet 1989). In more recent years, some further refinements were made to the approach (Paquet 1999, 2009, 2013; Paquet and Wilson 2012). This chapter presents a very succinct and synthetic version of this exploratory work to define a process of inquiry and social learning. For a less elliptic presentation, the reader is invited to refer to the recent vintage of the literature mentioned.

mechanisms that will bring the system to the desired state. As a result, much time has been spent over the past 60 years forcing problems into such a mould. On the basis of this sort of simplification, based on a poor understanding of the real nature of the issues, targets are imagined and instruments like bows and arrows are proposed to ensure good marksmanship in hitting the targets.

This primitive approach remains the standard template in strategy and policy analysis in a large number of agencies, and in most segments of academe. It is built on many false presumptions that:

- the problem facing the organization is known and well-understood;
- the problem is well structured, and that the appropriate policy or strategy can be engineered in the same way a puzzle can be solved;
- someone is in charge and fully informed, and can determine the goals to be pursued; and
- the strategy is not only technically feasible, but also socially acceptable, implementable and not too politically destabilizing.

If and when all these presumptions are in place, the traditional approach works well. But when these presumptions are unwarranted, adjustments to the methods of inquiry are required. When the problems are ill-structured (i.e., without well-defined goals and well-defined constraints), operations research methods do not fit the bill. What is called for is continuous feedback between problem formulation and quasi-analytic methods that are more process-oriented than outcome-oriented. The difference between ends and means, and between the policy objectives and the social technology, that is set up to pursue them, are blurred (Ansoff 1960). The guidance system must become an *inquiring and learning system* that is self-organizing to a great extent (Vickers 1965), and depends much on what John Dewey would have called *experimental intelligence* and socially organized intelligence (Dewey 1935: chapter 3).

Such an alternative approach allows strategy and policy to avoid the toxic Manichean choice of either trying to fit the problems into unsatisfactory formal moulds designed for well-structured problems, or having to rely on the strictly intuitive approaches fit for totally unstructured problems.

The construction of a middle-of-the-road approach capable of dealing effectively with ill-structured problems has evolved very slowly because of the intellectually pleasing nature of the simplistic operations research approach. This is the case even though this primitive approach has tended to become more and more surreal as the increasing degree of complexity and wickedness of real-life problems made its formalist gymnastics less and less relevant to the practical world.

This chapter frontally attacks the hyper-stylization bent of the approach in good currency. The intent is to start from the basic premise that we live in a world where problems are more and more ill-structured and wicked (Paquet 1991), and where the presumptions mentioned above do not apply. Consequently, inquiring means: (1) that one has to recognize that goals, preferences and aspirations have to be discovered and learned; (2) that such social learning can usually proceed only through experimentation, prototyping and serious play with prototypes, and that this calls for intellectual processes that are quite different from the simple hypothesis testing proposed by positivism; (3) that this process of inquiring through learning-by-doing entails making the highest and best use of Delta knowledge; and (4) that strategy and policy pose less a question of decision than a question of effective design of inquiring systems as a way of generating effective wayfinding for organizations.

Since the traditional approach remains so well embedded in the culture, there is no need to spend time developing its presentation here, or reiterating the list of its inadequacies. The following pages will focus much more on sketching the contours of the sort of alternative way to conduct inquiries, capable of successfully meeting the challenges facing administration as a professional practice.

Inquiring into the practice of administration

The old primitive way to deal with strategy and policy was based on a rather static view of the world: the problem definition is caricatured as a puzzle that calls for a solution. The new alternative way has to be more dynamic. It accepts that the nature of the problem is ill-defined to start with, and evolving as circumstances change and time goes by. This means that, as the problem definition evolves so must the very nature of ends and means, and even the nature of the organization. Neither means nor ends, nor the nature of the organization is a given.

This sort of dynamic is well captured in the path-breaking 1971 book, *Beyond the Stable State* by Donald Schön. In this book, Schön chronicles the loss of the stable state, and redefines *governing as designing a learning system*. In the following decade, Schön was to write two additional books that were meant to provide suggestions as to how the reflective practitioner might be able to respond effectively to the challenges of governance as social learning (Schön 1983, 1987).

The intent in this chapter is to reconstruct, along this line, the practice of administration as a dynamic process of social learning, to expose some of the mechanisms through which this sort of social learning unfolds, and to underline some of the important costs attached to the failure to take full advantage of the sort of tacit and implicit learning that is at the core of social learning.

This reconstruction proceeds in five steps. First, *delta knowledge* is defined as a central feature in the work of the reflective practitioner in the professional work of administration. This leads to an exploration of what sort of cognitive processes underpin the acquisition of delta knowledge, and the mix of *savoirs, savoir-faire* and *savoir-être* required in professional practice. Second, two important features of administration as a practice are probed in a preliminary way: the process of *transduction* that underpins it, and the process of *connoisseurship as tacit knowledge* that is embodied in the practice of the reflective practitioner. Thirdly, both transduction and connoisseurship are shown to have a fundamental social character; and social learning as a process to constitute a third way – the way of the reflective practitioner – a middle-of-the-road strategy between the model of technical rationality and the nihilism of those who claim that there is no discernible dominant logic at work in administration. Fourthly, it is suggested that the reflective practitioner operates best in local worlds, and the parallel processes through which the reflective practitioner carries out his inquiry in the new approach designed to deal with ill-structured and wicked problems are sketched. In closing, I hint at the sort of intellectual toolbox of capacities that should be added when training managers and administrators. The current nature of training appears to be inadequate and is a major source of coordination failures and poor governance.

Delta knowledge

Many different methods of subdividing knowledge have been proposed over time – from Aristotle (1999) (intelligence of first principles, theoretical, practical, productive) to Fritz Machlup's *Knowledge: Its Creation, Distribution, and Economic Significance* in the 1980s (where the higher classes of knowledge are labelled humanistic, scientific and social-science). Each of these taxonomies suggests different forms of knowledge for which there is a cognate learning activity. But most of these taxonomies are deficient because of their restrictive focus on formal knowledge: they neglect all sorts of *other forms of knowledge* as mundane, unwholesome, unwanted, illusive, etc. To highlight this deficiency (because these other forms of knowledge are fundamentally important to the understanding of creativity, entrepreneurship and innovation in a knowledge economy), I have suggested the creation of a new generic and inclusive category of knowledge that focuses on this other sort of knowledge.

Using as a starting point something very close to the Machlup classification of types of higher knowledge (Machlup 1980), I have attached the labels that used to be in good currency in Dutch university circles to identify these types of knowledge. In the Netherlands, the university faculties in which humanistic knowledge, scientific knowledge, and social-science knowledge are generated are called *alpha, beta and gamma*, respectively (HOOP 1987).

It is obvious that the terrain occupied by these categories of knowledge does not exhaust the whole domain of knowledge. Much of what exists in the form of ordinary knowledge is excluded from these *emplacements*. All sorts of aspects of making and doing – "wroughting and wrighting," in the language of Bruce Archer (1978) – are forms of knowledge excluded from the traditional triad. This knowledge, generated by and for wroughting and wrighting, is what we have labelled the territory of *delta knowledge* (Gilles and Paquet 1989).

The *delta* territory is the world of practical philosophy, the world of reflection in action. The contours of this world may be gauged by reference to the aims and activities of the Royal Society for the Encouragement of Arts, Manufactures, and Commerce, founded in 1754 by William Shipley. It starts with the practical as opposed to the theoretical, thereby turning on its head the basic epistemology of technical rationality that is embedded in the branches of knowledge production in good currency in the social sciences these days (Schön 1983).

The prevailing "technical rationality model" in science and social science presumes that everything flows from basic science or its underlying disciplines; basic principles derived from basic science are then applied to problem-solutions and real-life procedures, before they find their way to the service of clients. This cascading of knowledge production presumes that there is a one-way street from the theoretical to the practical. This linear model may be regarded as dead, but it won't lie down.

In reality, knowledge may emanate from reflection in action: for example, professional work in medicine is not applied biology. Being conditioned by tradition and inheritance, successful progress in knowledge production may emanate from trial and error. As Arthur Koestler has noted, "the revolutions in the history of science are successful escapes from blind alleys. The evolution of knowledge is continuous only during those periods of consolidation and elaboration which follow a major breakthrough. Sooner or later, however, consolidation leads to increasing rigidity, orthodoxy and so into the dead end of overspecialization. Eventually there is a crisis and a new 'breakthrough' out of the blind alley ... and so the cycle starts again" (Koestler 1967: 168-9).

Schön has suggested that, for the professional, knowledge production proceeds in a way exactly obverse to the one suggested by the technical rationality model: it is the issue rather than the theory that comes first, and reflection-in-action is the technique that crafts new knowledge. In doing a job, the professional not only applies knowledge, but produces knowledge. Delta knowledge emerges from concerns for the particular, the local, the timely, and the oral (Toulmin 1988). It flows from a reflection on experience, a conversation with the situation. This is a situation best exemplified by the challenge faced by the designer: the need to search for some kind of harmony between two intangibles – a form which has not yet been designed, and a context that cannot be properly and fully described because it is still evolving (Alexander 1964).

Delta knowledge is different from knowledge produced via the scientific and social-scientific route.

First, it uses a very different methodology (heuristics) based on a very different epistemology (an epistemology of practice (Friedman 1978)). Secondly, it pertains to a domain excluded from the territory covered by the theory-centred approaches. Its focus is *know-how* and not *know-what*. Thirdly, the sort of knowledge acquired through learning-by-doing has important tacit and idiosyncratic components. This explains why the process of experimentation proceeds in some settings with enthusiasm, skill and persistence, while in other settings experimentation takes place only slowly and ineptly (Murnane and Nelson 1984: 5). Finally, the production of delta knowledge follows rules that are largely implicit, overlapping, diverse, variously applied, contextually dependent, and subject to exceptions and to critical modifications (Schön 1987, 1988).

Professional practice, transduction and connoisseurship

In the world of technical rationality, it has come to be believed that the ladder of abstraction goes from sensory data that provide repeated observations; from these replicated observations, associations emerge and are memorized. The knowledge gained by association is then generalized by inference to classes of objects, and associations between classes of objects, such as those of cause and effect. Knowledge is thus the accumulation of these tried and true associations. Education becomes merely the distribution of such tested, reliable accumulated knowledge (Emery 1980).

In the world of delta knowledge, critical thinking evolves not from content-free principles and methodologies, but from schemata that are highly specific to the task at hand, and that are not easily transferable from one task to the next. In the beginning, according to this approach, is perception (Polanyi 1958: 96). While the world of technical rationality teaches that one must distrust personal experience as a guide to knowledge – the goal is to produce a disciplined mind through exposure to the accumulation of proven knowledge – professional practice takes its roots in cognition that has its genesis in the perception and experience of the individual. Knowledge is thus restricted only by our habits of perception, so one must educate one's perceptual systems (Gibson 1979; Paquet 1989b).

As early as 1938, Chester Barnard introduced a distinction in the management literature between "thinking processes" and "non-logical processes," and insisted that the latter were omnipresent in effective professional practice (Barnard 1938). More recently, Henry Mintzberg insisted that administration is an activity that is based in large part on the development of perception and thinking with the right side of the brain – the locus of the implicit, of the experimental, of the synthetic. He has also often reiterated that strategies are not deduced, that they are crafted, that they "emerge" sometimes in unexpected form as a result of the confrontation with a reality that may or may not adopt it well (Mintzberg 1976, 1987).

At the core of this process of *crafting* is what Schön and Rein (1994) have called *design rationality*: it connotes the capacity to reflect systematically, rigorously and cumulatively *in action* as the inquiry proceeds. This is a process of *focused rational exploration* that is quite familiar in professional practice and design.

Since the problem is ill-structured to begin with, one must of necessity begin with the sort of exploration that Henri Lefebvre (1961) has called *experimental utopia* (*"l'exploration du possible humain avec l'aide de l'image et de l'imaginaire, accompagnée d'une incessante critique et d'une incessante référence à la problématique donnée dans le réel"*). This exploration is geared to the generation of a form that fits: it is a conversation with the situation, an interactive learning process. It calls for a cerebral operation that is quite different from both deduction and induction, and that Lefebvre has called *transduction*. The process of transduction *"construit ... un objet possible ... à partir d'informations portant sur la réalité ainsi que d'une problématique posée par cette réalité"* (Lefebvre 1961). This process of transduction characterizes many of the cases analyzed by Schön, and fits very well with his generalized notion of design rationality (Schön and Rein 1994: 167ff).

Through this process of accumulation and assimilation of evidence through conversation with the situation, the individual's diagnostic capability grows. This cumulative experience of the resolution of situated problems is the essence of *connoisseurship*; it is developed by relating and comparing within a field of knowledge (Freedberg 1989). It materializes through looking at a multiplicity of cases, describing examples, drawing analogies and drawing attention to the *intermediate cases* so that one can pass easily from familiar cases to the unfamiliar and see the relation between them (Tully 1995).

Connoisseurship, like skill, is communicated by experience and examples, not by precepts. One cannot develop an appreciation of human physiognomies except through a long course of experience – in much the same way that we acquire the skill of a wine-taster, or the capacity to swim or to ride a bicycle (Polanyi 1958: 54). There is no spontaneous emergence of connoisseurship. It emerges in action from the jointness of some basic capability, and from a very extensive external exposure to a large number of intermediate cases.

Connoisseurship can never be the result of the application of simple explicit rules. It is a *tacit savoir-faire* and *savoir-être,* and becomes part of the fabric of the trainee. Like skill, connoisseurship can only be communicated by example (*Ibid.:* 54). It instinctively generates a response in the face of complex and uncertain circumstances – a response that appropriately balances a number of complex incommensurable dimensions *hic et nunc,* in the way that the muscles of the eye adjust to the lens of a new pair of glasses (*Ibid.:* 97).

Learning in this context is like learning to swim. It is done by eliminating misfits, by correcting errors, by continuous re-alignment to ensure goodness-of-fit between elusive standards and circumstances. There can be no learning unless one recognizes and embraces error as a fundamental building block, as a crucial way to fuel fruitful deliberations. The new competences required in such learning systems only develop under certain conditions. There must be: (1) an explicit acknowledgement of the high level of uncertainty as completely irreducible; (2) an explicit will to embrace error as the difference between what is expected and what happens; and (3) a willingness to span boundaries across perspectives (Michael 1993).

We know from experience that sometimes learning faster is a matter of survival. Our immune system is constantly bombarded by new viruses, and it must learn and adapt quickly if we are to survive. At times, it may become necessary to use a vaccine: a lever to help it learn faster about the best way to fight a disease.

The same can be said about any complex adaptive system, be it a living company, à la Arie de Geus (1997), our large cities, or our socio-economy. In all these cases of complex adaptive social systems, it is likely to depend in critical times on a sort of stewardship that might be regarded as the equivalent of the vaccine *vis-à-vis* the immune system – i.e., a nexus of network or system stimulations that nudge and accelerate the process of learning (Paquet 1997).

The social practitioner as inquirer and explorer

Some decades ago, Friedmann and Abonyi (1976) stylized a simple *social learning exploratory model of policy research* to deal with wicked problems. They have suggested that it requires responding to four basic questions about any possible action plan: Is it technically feasible? Is it socially acceptable? Is it too politically destabilizing? Is it implementable? In order to respond to these questions, one requires some appreciation: (1) of appropriate theories of reality; (2) of the ways social values are expressed; (3) of the political game within which the design exercise is carried out; and (4) of the ways in which collective action is carried out. These four pillars of social learning are interconnected, and any change in one affects the others. This paradigm of social practice in policy research is synthesized in the figure reproduced below.

A social learning model of policy research

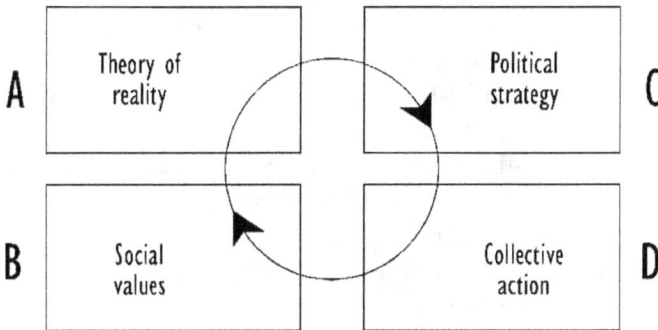

Source: Friedman and Abonyi, 1976, p. 934.

Block B is the locus of the nexus of the different value systems that provide normative guidance, either in the transformation of reality, or in the selection of strategies for action; theory of reality [block A] refers to a symbolic representation and explanation of the complex environment; political strategy [block C] connotes the political game which generates the course of action chosen; collective action [block D] deals with implementation and the interaction with partner groups. Together, these four components come to life in concrete situations.

Traditional approaches to policy research focus on attempts to falsify hypotheses about some objective reality, according to the canons of scientific experimentation. This is too narrow a focus for policy research when the ground is in motion. For *social practitioners* like Friedmann and Abonyi, what is central is an effort "to create a wholly new, unprecedented situation that, in its possibility for generating new knowledge, goes substantially beyond the initial hypothesis" (Friedmann and Abonyi 1976: 936). The social learning paradigm is built on reflection-in-action, dialogue, and mutual learning by experts and clients: i.e., on an interactive or trans-active style of planning. "The paradigm makes the important epistemological assumption that action hypotheses are verified as 'correct' knowledge only in the course of a social practice that includes the four components of theory (of reality), the configuration of values, strategy, and action. A further epistemological commitment is to the creation of a new reality, and hence to a new knowledge, rather than in establishing the truth-value of propositions in abstraction from the social context to which they are applied."[2] Similar general ideas have been explored over time by many others, including Carl Taylor (1997).

This social learning framework has been used most effectively in analyzing complex phenomena like multiculturalism (Paquet 2008). But this formulation of the social learning approach has not been sufficiently well operationalized, from the start, to foster wide adoption and extensive applications of this approach to the large number of wicked problems in need of such an approach. What has been missing is a more carefully spelled out version of this approach in order to make it more easily useable as a reference protocol for analysts interested in applying it to various issue domains.

---

[2] John Friedmann and George Abonyi, 1976. *op.cit.* p. 938; Donald A. Schön, 1983.

A recent book has attempted to fill that gap (Paquet 2013) and to sketch the contours of this sort of inquiring and exploration work in stages:

- one does not usually have *ab ovo* a good grasp of the situation;
- consequently, collaborative governance requires one to start with a process of inquiry to ascertain the *state of affairs,* and to gather the necessary information that is spread widely among stakeholders and potential partners;
- most potential partners have no shared values or common purposes, and no one has all the information, resources, and power to fully take charge and to guide the organization in ways assuring resilience and innovation, so what must be constructed are arenas or symbolic platforms where these diverse perspectives can be blended into a more or less viable *evolving synoptic perspective;*
- the inquiring system and the blending of perspectives are *necessary* to elicit a mix of principles, conventions, rules, and mechanisms to ensure effective coordination, and to construct the equivalent of an automatic pilot to generate wayfinding, resilience, and innovativeness, but they are *not sufficient* conditions;
- the infrastructure of social learning must also be in place to feed the exploration and the probing through the detection and correction of incongruities as the organization proceeds through the social learning cycle;
- it is naïve to pretend that the collaborative governance emerging in this manner will necessarily be able to resist and survive in the face of failure and tough times. It will be essential to ensure the development of *negative capability*: the capability to keep going when things are going wrong, through the operations of safe-fail and fail-safe mechanisms, and other ways of sustaining commitment.

This approach[3] is meant to immunize the inquiring system against the false sense of virtue in decisiveness that leads so many to take action prematurely, and with undue haste, before a good grasp of the situation is gained. Not only is this undue haste likely to be both myopic, and not to embrace the full range of possibilities, but it is also likely to sabotage the nurturing and maintaining of the commitment of partners by falling prey to an undue *urgence de conclure.*

Conflicting frames and circumscribed settings

The reflective practitioner, whether part of a firm or of a state or community agency, is embedded in a knowledge system, a complex web of systemic relationships among suppliers, customers, partners, etc., who co-create value through their interactions. These relations underpin an intricate and complex network of collaboration in an integrated value-creating system in which much of the knowledge is tacit knowledge (Wikstrom and Normann 1994). This complex web of relationships that makes up the modern organization is a nexus of contracts (formal and informal, legal and moral, etc.) and it translates into various capabilities.

One of the most important features of a learning system is its capacity to speed up the rate of learning. Administration as transduction is a professional practice of 'localized' social learning at the core of the organization. It is a form of connoisseurship, of practical wisdom that acts as a lever for learning. Even though it is bound to take very different forms depending on the socio-cultural underground in which the learning organization is embedded, it represents everywhere an on-going capacity to maintain, aggrandize and innovate on a day-to-day basis as part of reflection in action (Schön and Rein 1994).

Hampden-Turner and Trompenaars (1993) have shown in a survey of 15,000 senior private sector managers and

---

[3] This is not the only approach developed to tackle wicked problems. A most interesting and rich approach is the one developed by Brown, Harris, and Russell (eds.) in *Tackling Wicked Problems: Through the Transdisciplinary Imagination* (2010).

administrators how different their value systems may be from country to country, and how administration may therefore vary immensely according to cultures. Hall and Hall (1987) have shown that often the single greatest barrier to effective administrative success is the one erected by culture. This underlines, if there is still a need to do so, the fundamentally social dimension of administration as professional practice.

This explains why "when policy controversies are abstracted from the situations in which they arise, as in academic discourse, ... they exist in a kind of vacuum where it is hard to imagine how they might ever be resolved... when policy controversies are situated in the fruitful mire of an actual policy area, a great variety of processes open up and many different kinds of outcome become possible" (Schön and Rein 1994: 176). This is the case because the inquirers have an overriding interest in getting something done, the situated debate provides much informational richness, and because each actor is forced to interact and communicate with the others. In contrast, when the problem definition and the policy are not situated, there is no compulsion to engage in co-design, and there is a lack of the aids to communication that co-design provides (*Ibid.*: 178). Moreover, situated frame reflection creates a behavioural world more conducive to mutual trust and to engaging in reciprocal reflection than the usual bureaucratic and political climate that is more likely to breed mutual suspicion. In that sense, a situated policy controversy among conflicting frames provides a greater chance that speculation will generate a choice among frames or a blend of frames based on fruitfulness (*Ibid.*: 44).

Delta knowledge and exploration capabilities

Delta knowledge is not a new phenomenon. It can be easily linked to the form of intelligence and knowledge that the Greek philosophers called *metis*, and that connotes *"un ensemble complexe, mais très cohérent, d'attitudes mentales, de comportements intellectuels qui combinent le flair, la sagacité, la prévision, la souplesse d'esprit, la feinte, la débrouillardise, l'attention vigilante, le sens de l'opportunité, des habiletés diverses, une expérience longuement acquise; elle s'applique à des réalités fugaces, mouvantes, déconcertantes, ambiguës, qui ne se prêtent ni à la mesure précise, ni au calcul exact, ni au raisonnement rigoureux"* (Detienne and Vernant 1974). Isaiah Berlin (1953) celebrated the *metis* of the fox which has a variety of tricks, and compared it to the *techne* of the hedgehog who has only one trick in the face of danger: rolling itself into a ball with its quills on the outside.

Aristotle is probably the philosopher who has provided the most subtle analysis of this form of knowledge. He observed that while animals are capable of *metis*, humans are superior because they are capable of a melange of *metis* and *phronesis*. For him, the challenges posed by complex situations (to which simple rules offer no response) call for *phronesis* (practical wisdom). It is not simply the right understanding or the capacity to assess action correctly, but it is the union of good judgment and the action which is the fitting embodiment of that judgment (Beiner 1983).

This reflection-in-action requires a conversation with the situation. It is a social act; it is the result of argumentation – among particular people, in specific situations, dealing with concrete things, with different things at stake (Toulmin 1988). Deliberation and argumentation are possible only within the community of stakeholders, of those affected and concerned. Thus, delta knowledge as *embodied savoir-faire* does not materialize through the process of abstraction. It materializes via a social process which resembles the one through which a child learns a complex practical system like a language.

Because it is built on a conversation with the situation, and communication and deliberation with the community of stakeholders, *phronesis* is a form of *prudential connoisseurship* built on a process of social learning. And professional practice, be it as a designer or as an administrator, is nothing but a form of localized social learning within an organization which is, itself, a knowledge system and a learning system, adapting in part to its circumstances and being adopted in part by its broad environment.

In the range of capabilities, one might distinguish those that are rooted in forms of knowledge that are idiosyncratically synergistic, inimitable, and non-contestable – the *intrinsic core capabilities* – and those that are easily imitable and contestable – the *ancillary capabilities* (Langlois and Robertson 1995). Such capabilities are obviously *capable of being increased, augmented and enriched*. This may be done more or less well, depending on the greater or lesser ability of the organization at learning (learning by doing, learning by learning, etc.), and at picking up information from external sources (absorptive capacity). But there may also be a failure to learn through inertia, laziness, or through blockages limiting absorptive capacity.

Conclusion

What is most important is the development of *a new frame of mind* which leads to approaching organizations not only in an *inquiring mode*, but also with a *design attitude*.

Inquiring and designing are a conversation with the situation that leads to experimenting with rules and guideposts. This, in turn, reveals conflicts and dilemmas in the appreciative system. Since participants talk across discrepant frames, explorative inquiring and designing leads to learning by doing. This entails a shift from the *exploitation* of existing knowledge to *exploration* for new knowledge: from routine management to the continuous reinvention of the organization, and from short-term and low-risk to long-term and high-risk undertakings (March 1991, Martin 2009).

Over the past 20 years, the well-entrenched *problematiques* have robustly resisted the invasion of this new paradigm. This is not surprising, since there is much resilient power in the sort of dynamic conservatism of those whose total intellectual capital is invested in the old ways. Yet the cost of the governance failures that are thereby denied instead of repaired is becoming sufficiently large for many to be concerned.

References

Alexander, Christopher. 1964. *Notes toward a Synthesis of Form.* Cambridge, MA: Harvard University Press.

Ansoff, H. Igor. 1960. "A quasi-analytic method for long-range planning" in C.W. Churchman and M. Verulst (eds.). *Management Sciences – Models and Techniques.* London, UK: Pergamon Press.

Archer, Bruce. 1978. *Time for a Revolution in Arts and Design Education.* London, UK: Royal College of Art Papers, No. 6.

Aristotle. 1999. *Nicomachean Ethics.* Book VI. Kitchener, ON: Batoche Books.

Barnard, Chester. 1938. *The Functions of the Executive.* Cambridge, MA: Harvard University Press.

Beiner, Ronald. 1983. *Political Judgment.* Chicago, IL: University of Chicago Press.

Berlin, Isaiah. 1953. *The Hedgehog and the Fox.* London, UK: Weidenfeld & Nicolson.

Brown, Valerie A., John A. Harris, and Jacqueline Y. Russell (eds.). 2010. *Tackling Wicked Problems: Through the Transdisciplinary Imagination.* London, UK: Earthscan.

de Geus, Arie. 1997. "The Living Company," *Harvard Business Review,* 75(2): 51-59.

Detienne, Marcel and Jean-Pierre Vernant. 1974. *Les ruses de l'intelligence.* Paris: Flammarion.

Dewey, John. 1935. *Liberalism and Social Action.* New York, NY: Putnam.

Emery, Frank. 1980. *Educational Paradigms – An Epistemological Revolution.* mimeo.

Freedberg, S.J. 1989. "Berenson, Connoisseurship and the History of Art," *The New Criterion,* 7(6): 7-16.

Friedmann, John. 1978. "The Epistemology of Practice: A Critique of Objective Knowledge," *Theory and Society,* 6(1): 75-92.

Friedmann, John and George Abonyi. 1976. "Social Learning: A Model for Policy Research," *Environment and Planning*, A, 8(8): 927-940.

Gibson, J.J. 1979. *The Ecological Approach to Visual Perception.* Boston, MA: Houghton-Mifflin.

Gilles, Willem and Gilles Paquet. 1989. "On Delta Knowledge," in G. Paquet and M. von Zur-Muehlen (eds.). *Edging Toward the Year 2000.* Ottawa, ON: Canadian Federation of Deans of Management and Administrative Studies, p. 1-30.

Hall, E.T. and Mildred R. Hall. 1987. *Hidden Differences.* New York: Anchor Books/Doubleday.

Hampden-Turner, Charles and Alfons Trompenaars. 1993. *The Seven Cultures of Capitalism.* New York, NY: Currency/Doubleday.

HOOP. 1987. *Kerndocument Hoger Onderwijs en Onderzoek (HOOP) Plan 1.* Zoetermeer, NL: Ministerie van Onderwijs en Wetenschappen.

Koestler, Arthur. 1967. *The Ghost in the Machine.* New York, NY: Macmillan.

Langlois, Richard N. and Paul L. Robertson. 1995. *Firms, Markets and Economic Change.* London, UK: Routledge.

Lefebvre, Henri. 1961. "Utopie expérimentale: pour un nouvel urbanisme," *Revue francaise de sociologie*, 2(3).

Machlup, Fritz. 1980/1982/1984. *Knowledge: Its Creation, Distribution, and Economic Significance.* Princeton, NJ: Princeton University Press, Volumes I, II, III.

March, James G. 1991. "Exploration and Exploitation in Organizational Learning," *Organization Science*, 2: 71-87.

Martin, Roger. 2009. *The Design of Business.* Boston, MA: Harvard Business Press.

Michael, Donald N. 1993 "Governing by Learning: Boundaries, Myths and Metaphors," *Futures*, January-February, p. 81-89.

Mintzberg, Henry. 1976. "Planning on the Left Side and Managing on the Right," *Harvard Business Review*, July-August, p. 49-58.

Mintzberg, Henry. 1987. "Crafting Strategy," *Harvard Business Review*, July-August, p. 66-75.

Murnane, R.J. and R.R. Nelson. 1984. "Production and Innovation When Techniques are Tacit," *Journal of Economic Behavior and Organization*.

Paquet, Gilles. 1971. "Social Science Research as an Evaluative Instrument for Social Policy," in G.E. Nettler and K. Krotki (eds.). *Social Science and Social Policy*. Edmonton, AB: Human Resources Research Council, p. 49-66.

Paquet, Gilles. 1989a. "A Social Learning Framework for a Wicked Problem: The Case of Energy," *Energy Studies Review*, 1(1): 55-69.

Paquet, Gilles. 1989b. "Liberal Education as Synecdoche," in C. Andrew and S.B. Esbensen (eds.). *Who's Afraid of Liberal Education?* Ottawa, ON: University of Ottawa Press, p. 1-20.

Paquet, Gilles. 1991. "Policy as Process: Tackling Wicked Problems," in T.J. Courchene and A.E. Stewart (eds.). *Essays on Canadian Public Policy*, Kingston, ON: Queen's University School of Policy Studies, p. 171-186.

Paquet, Gilles. 1997. "The Burden of Office, Ethics and Connoisseurship," *Canadian Public Administration*, 40(1): 55-71.

Paquet, Gilles. 1999. *Governance through Social Learning*. Ottawa, ON: University of Ottawa Press.

Paquet, Gilles. 2008. *Deep Cultural Diversity – A Governance Challenge*. Ottawa, ON: University of Ottawa Press.

Paquet, Gilles. 2009. *Scheming virtuously: The road to collaborative governance*, Ottawa, ON: Invenire Books.

Paquet, Gilles. 2013. *Tackling Wicked Policy Problems: Equality, Diversity and Sustainability*. Ottawa, ON: Invenire Books.

Paquet, Gilles and Christopher Wilson. 2012, "Inquiring Systems," in R. Hubbard, G. Paquet, and C. Wilson. *Stewardship*. Ottawa, ON: Invenire Books, p. 31-54.

Polanyi, Michael. 1958. *Personal Knowledge*. Chicago, IL: University of Chicago Press.

Schön, Donald A. 1971. *Beyond the Stable State*. New York, NY: Norton.

Schön, Donald A. 1983. *The Reflective Practitioner*. New York, NY: Basic Books.

Schön, Donald A. 1987 *Educating the Reflective Practitioner*. San Francisco, CA: Jossey-Bass.

Schön, Donald A. 1988. "Designing: Rules, Types and Worlds," *Design Studies*, 9(3): 181-190.

Schön, Donald A. and Martin Rein. 1994. *Frame Reflection – Toward the Resolution of Intractable Policy Controversies*. New York, NY: Basic Books.

Taylor, Carl A. 1997. "The ACIDD Test: a framework for policy planning and decision-making," *Optimum*, 27(4): 53-62.

Toulmin, Stephen. 1988. "The Recovery of Practical Philosophy," *The American Scholar*, 47(3): 337-352.

Tully, James. 1995. *Strange Multiplicity*. Cambridge, UK: Cambridge University Press.

Vickers, Geoffrey. 1965. *The Art of Judgment*. London, UK: Chapman & Hall.

Wikstrom, Solveig and Richard Normann. 1994. *Knowledge and Value: A New Perspective on Corporate Transformation*. London, UK: Routledge.

PART II

On Exorcizing Pathologies

I have underlined in Part I the fact that mental prisons are important blockages in the process of inquiring, and that difficulties in communication and interaction among groups with different perspectives are also important impediments to social learning.

There is no way that the whole range of mental prisons and interaction breakdowns that have stunted social learning can be exposed in a few pages. Therefore I have selected one particular instance of each of these two families of blockages – quantophrenia as a mental prison, and disloyalty as a crucial failure in the process of collaboration that is central in effective governance – as a way to illustrate how such pathologies create significant difficulties in the process of social learning and are responsible for governance failures.

In chapter 3, I denounce the quantophrenic cosmology that claims that only quantitative information is relevant and meaningful. This approach is an echo of a crippling epistemology. It generates a reductive view of the world, inspires much ill-inspired actions, and may be regarded as an important source of poor governance. A less reductive and more modest approach would appear to be more promising.

In chapter 4, I examine the nebulas of loyalty and disloyalty especially as they are experienced at the interface between elected officials and bureaucrats. The same difficulties exist in the private and social sectors, but they appear more 'clear cut' and stylized in the public sector. While the real-life experience at the political-bureaucratic interface cannot usefully be characterized most of the time in terms of blind loyalty or treasonous disloyalty, operating in the no-man's land between these poles creates a very daunting challenge. It is necessary to reflect on what might be a useful philosophical map to guide action.

In both cases, the distorting mental prisons generated by crippling epistemologies, and the disjunctive factors sabotaging effective collaboration, are important sources of failures in both social learning and governance. While there is no miracle cure – we all suffer to some extent from biases in our inquiring, and our collaborative relations are never completely free of questioning – both families of difficulties cannot reasonably be presumed to be non-existent, and call for much critical thinking, if the malefits they generate are to be neutralized to the maximum extent possible.

CHAPTER 3
| On Quantophrenia[1]

"If it cannot be measured, it cannot be controlled ..."
Lord Kelvin

"Not everything that counts, can be counted, and not everything
that can be counted, counts ..."
Albert Einstein

"It is better to solve the right problem the wrong way than to
solve the wrong problem the right way."
Richard Hamming

Introduction

This chapter addresses some concerns raised by Pitirim
Sorokin some 50 years ago (Sorokin 1956). At the time,
Sorokin was somewhat distraught by the social sciences
falling prey to all sorts of manias and foibles – mindless
application of the methods in use in the experimental sciences
to social sciences issues, sterile formalization, useless number-
crunching, and the like – that were in danger of derailing socio-

[1] This is a revised version of a paper delivered at a breakfast meeting debate
organized by the IPAC Toronto Regional Chapter at Victoria College
(University of Toronto) on November 18, 2008 on the general topic of
measurable results and public policy. The kindness of Amanda Parr, the
architect of this event, and the courteous intellectual provocation of my
colleague Ralph Heintzman have been immensely appreciated.

economic inquiries away from the purposes that had given rise to the social sciences to begin with: that is to respond to *une fringale de sens*.

Sorokin's book attacked a variety of pathologies, but spent two chapters on what he called quantophrenia.

It should be clear that Sorokin's attacks were not directed at quantification *per se*. Quantitative methods have been used from time immemorial as powerful instruments of reasoning. The problem arises when the use of such tools becomes the basis of a *cult*, roughly captured by the motto that if it cannot be measured, it does not exist. Such a cult distorts the appreciation we have of socio-economic phenomena, and this mental prison acts as blinders that have toxic unintended consequences for public policies when they are shaped by an apparatus thus constrained.

Sorokin's *mise en garde* generated some prudence in the use of quantitative methods in most social sciences, as experience revealed the deleterious nature of this cult, and as it has become clear, over time, that crippling epistemologies generate governance failures (Paquet 2009a).

Public management (and management in general) has for a long time resisted this sort of contamination, but it has been infected by numerology in recent decades. Reading Chester Barnard (1938), Herbert Simon (1947) or Geoffrey Vickers (1965), one might not have anticipated that management studies would become obsessed by quantification as a result of the viral influence of operations research. But it has happened.

Crippling epistemologies and policy pseudo-sciences

Quite sensibly, Sorokin ascribes the propensity to *quantulate* to some fundamental deficiencies at the philosophical and epistemological levels.

It all began with the quasi-theological fundamentalism echoed by words like *objectivity* or *truth* when they began to serve as references in the mushy world of public administration. Under the influence of Emile Durkheim and others, it was argued that *"les faits sociaux sont des choses,"* and that one should generalize the application to them of the sort of scientistic methods in use in the physical sciences.

This percolated, after quite a lag, into the promises of the so-called 'policy sciences,' erected on the model of management science. Those policy sciences are based on the presumption that public, private and social organizations are directed by omniscient leaders who have a good understanding of their environments, of the future trends in that environment if nothing were done to modify it, of the inexorable rules of the game they have to put up with, and of the goals pursued by their own organizations.

Policy sciences were, and are, starkly *Newtonian*. They postulate a deterministic, well-behaved world, where causality is simple because the whole is the sum of the parts. Given the well-defined goals of the organization, and the more or less placid environment, the challenge is purported to be the design of control mechanisms likely to get the organization to where it wants to be. Many issues were and still are tractable with this approach, but most are not.

In the last few decades, the pace of change has accelerated and the issues have grown more complex. Private, public and social organizations have been confronted more and more with *wicked* problems (Paquet 1999: chapter 2). In this *quantum* sort of world, there is no objective reality, the uncertainty principle looms large, events are at best probable, and the whole is a network of synergies and interactions among the different parts of the system that is quite different from the sum of the parts (Becker 1991). To deal with these wicked problems, a new way of thinking about governing is required.

In this quantum world, *nobody is fully in charge* (Cleveland 2002). This has forced the governing system to evolve. It has been transformed (through a number of rounds of adaptation over the years) so as to accommodate the presence of multiple stakeholders, to respond to a plurality of groups in possession of part of the resources, the power and the information, and to provide the requisite flexibility and suppleness of action.

The ultimate result of these changes is a multi-stakeholder governance system built on unreliable control mechanisms, in pursuit of ill-defined goals, in a universe that is chronically in a state of flux.

When dealing with such a universe in a reasonable and practical way, the scientistic apparatus proves pretentious and inadequate, and Fukuyama (2004) could recently refer to the 'black hole of public administration' without generating much outraged reaction.

In this world of small g network-governance (that has replaced the world of top-down big G Government) – labels that apply equally well to organizations in the private, public and social sectors – organizations govern themselves by becoming capable of learning both new goals and new means *as they proceed*. This can only be done through tapping into the knowledge and information of all the citizens, but also by ensuring the collaboration of members of the organization that have a relevant portion of the resources, power or information, and by allowing them to invent ways out of the predicaments they are in (Sullivan and Skelcher 2002; McCarthy *et al.* 2004; Parker and Gallagher 2007; Bradwell and Reeves 2008).

Such a governance system deprives so-called leaders of any illusion that they have a monopoly on the governing of the organization. For the organization to learn fast, everyone must take part in the 'conversation,' and bring forward each bit of knowledge and wisdom that he or she has that may have a bearing on the issue (Paquet 1999, 2005). We are in a world of governing by experimenting and prototyping, of "governing by learning" (Michael 1993).

This process of social learning requires new governance structures (more modular, network-like, and integrated informal moral contracts). Yet this is only one half of the learning process. The other half is the work of stewardship. Instead of building on the assumption that the leader is omniscient, and is autocratically guiding top-down, the new distributed governance process builds on the critical dialogue with the stakeholders, ensuring that everyone learns about the nature of the problem, and about the consequences of various possible alternative initiatives (Paquet 2008a).

The citizenry learns in this manner to limit unreasonable demands; managers and administrators learn to listen and consult; other stakeholders learn enough about one another's views and interests to gauge the range of compromise solutions that are likely to prove acceptable and workable. The distributed governance process predicated on social learning builds on the answers to four questions posed to all stakeholders: Is it feasible? Is it socially acceptable? Is it too destabilizing politically? Can it be implemented? (Friedmann and Abonyi 1976; Taylor 1997).

This is the world of public policy in which the essential fuzziness of goals and targets and the essential uncertainty of means-ends relationships force the adoption of the social learning mode, a strategy of learning by doing, of learning by monitoring.

Whatever may be done to improve this process of learning must therefore be applauded: (1) the more outcome-oriented the focus of the conversation; (2) the more timely and performance-related the reporting/monitoring processes; and (3) the shorter the learning loops, the more effective the social learning process. It is not a matter of objectivity, truth, or testing of hypotheses, but a matter of experimenting, designing mechanisms, and disclosing and designing new worlds (Spinosa *et al.* 1997; Paquet 2008a, 2008b; Hubbard and Paquet 2009).

Words of caution about the quantophrenic cosmology

The public policy process as a social system is composed of three elements: structure, technology and theory. The structure consists of the set of roles and responsibilities of, and relations among, the actors involved in this process: citizens, stakeholders, officials, etc. The technology refers to the tools used by these actors. The theory is the view held by members about the process, its purposes, environment and future. These dimensions hang together, and any change in one affects the others (Schön 1971).

The capacity to transform is a measure of the organizational learning: the speed with which the public policy process is able to ensure the requisite restructuring, retooling, and reframing in order to enhance its triple-E performance: effectiveness (doing the right thing), efficiency (doing it right), and economy (doing it spartanly) while carefully maintaining due process and fairness, not only in the outcomes, but also in the very process through which these outcomes are generated.

One might usefully stylize the public policy process as a funnel – a funnel that ranges from a broad taking into account of the socio-technical environment to be regulated, through the mediating lenses of ideology, culture, institutions, and the structure of power, toward program definition, and service delivery.

The new 'quantophrenic cosmology' has tended to somewhat simplify this very complex public policy process, and to approach it in a rather parsimonious way: (1) by truncating the policy process and zooming in on the sub-process of delivery of services; and (2) by focusing within the service delivery segment mainly on the way to clarifying goals, and to sharpen reporting/monitoring indicators to increase, through clarity and transparency, the efficiency of the delivery process.

This approach has undoubtedly proved useful in some cases at the service delivery end of the public policy funnel – for example, measuring how much time it takes to have cheques mailed and delivered – and improving this sub-process. It is less clear what this clarification/reporting improvement is contributing or may contribute at the other end of the funnel – i.e., at the environment scanning/policy formation end of the spectrum.

However, the prophets of the new cosmology suggest that the clarification/reporting improvements hold the key to much more than the simple efficiency of the service delivery. This approach, we are told, will soon guide the conduct of the different programs, and determine the appropriateness of the allocation of roles and relationships in these programs. We are even promised that, through an aggregation of these local and partial measures (as building blocks), macro-machines will soon emerge generating indicators of performance for whole departments, and even for whole provincial or federal governments. Indeed, there are already prototypes of such mega-models and mega-measures being developed in the bowels of the Treasury Board Secretariat. The tail will soon wag the dog.

This ambitious new cosmology runs into difficulties: one danger, one seduction and one quagmire.

The danger of an overly sanitized stylization of the public policy process

The new cosmology has boldly sanitized the public policy process. The goals are presumed to be known and certain, the means-ends relationships clear, and the business plans transparent. This stylization sideswipes away many of the complexities of the multi-stakeholder power game that underpins much of public policy formation. It flies in the face not only of the day-to-day experience of any Ottawa watcher, but even of the stylization of the public policy process that is presented to would-be policy-makers by the official Canada School of Public Service (Smith and Taylor 1996).

The new cosmology excises the political haggling and the socio-technical milieu from the world of public management. This view of the public policy process tends to suggest: (a) the separability of the different phases of the policy process – policy formation, program design and delivery mechanism; (b) the sacred nature of the Westminster model of government, and the consequent assumption that accountability to the Minister must remain untouched as the process is amended; and (c) the presumption that explicit detailed contracts are sufficient to ensure that the policy intended by the senior executives (political and bureaucratic) will be carried out. All this represents an idealized world.

When it is suggested that what may be gathered from examining the service delivery portion of the policy funnel carries results that may be regarded as generalizeable to the whole policy funnel, one may reasonably claim that it is a *non sequitur*. The production of useful but limited observations, that are merrily blended into broader aggregates may not constitute meaningful syncretic summaries of the performance of a whole cluster of arrangements as they are based on the light generated by only a few flickering *clignotants*.[2]

The seduction of quantophrenia

The greatest appeal of the new quantophrenic cosmology is that it is not only built on an ideal-type of public policy as rational decision making, and reductively focuses on service delivery, but that it is also a *numerical* model. Goals, targets, outcomes and results are quantifiable, and performance indicators are to be computed to ensure that what has been promised can be compared to what has been realized. This is meant to bolster the legitimacy and credibility of the stylized policy process.

This numerical magic transmogrifies reality into a numerical representation, and performance into a set of *clignotants*. This fixation gives a false impression of certainty, and unduly simplifies a notion of performance that is essentially fuzzy. In fact, performance in public policy-making is an essentially contested concept.

W.B. Gallie has characterized a whole range of concepts as "essentially contested concepts ... the proper use of which inevitably involves endless disputes about their proper uses on the part of the users" (Gallie 1964: 158), and he has identified five conditions for a concept to be essentially contested. According to him, it must be: (1) appraisive, in the sense that it accredits some kind of valued achievement; (2) this achievement must be complex in character and its worth attributed to it as a whole; but (3) variously describable in its parts, with the possibility of various components being assigned more or less importance; and (4) open in character to the extent that it admits to considerable modification in the light of changing circumstances. Moreover, to qualify as an essentially contested

---

[2] Defined as turn signal, indicator; warning light/signal/sign. http://french. about.com/od/vocabulary/g/clignotant.htm.

concept, (5) each party must recognize that its own use of the concept is contested by other parties, and that the concept can be used both aggressively and defensively (*Ibid.*: 161).

A good example of such a concept might be 'championship' in a sport like figure skating, which can be judged in a number of different ways, with differential attention being paid to method, strategy, style, etc.

While the massaging of numbers probably provides much intellectual satisfaction to the massagers, the process easily degenerates into an exercise in the management of a numerical representation of reality, rather than the governance of reality.

Again, it must be restated that there is nothing inherently wrong about quantifying anything that can meaningfully be quantified. The downside of the quantophrenic cosmology is underlined when quantification is a camouflage – or verges on being a mystification – because it is used to sweep under the carpet unpleasant (because tractable only with great difficulty) issues while focusing attention on a reductive vision of the policy process. This is not unlike the pretenses of those naïve psephologists claiming to give an adequate account of politics and political behaviour through counting votes, or pretending to build meteorology "on elaborate computations of the flutterings of flags" (Andreski 1974: 132).

The quagmire of performance evaluation

This sacralization of numerology generates a real danger that such an essentially contested world might trigger whimsical measurements and perverse adjustments to them. Scoreboards and social indicators of performance become the dimensions steering the game, and agents adjust their behaviour accordingly. And, since whatever sets of indicators chosen are bound to be partial and imperfect, social learning may be misguided, slowed down, or even derailed.

These numerical indicators are bound to attract the attention of auditors and can steer organizations in unproductive ways, whatever the fragility of such indicators. This has been observed most dramatically in the world of 'phynance' (so spelled so as to remind all of its shamanic quality) where failing to meet quarterly sales or profit forecasts can generate disastrous results, whatever the soundness of the organizations from an economic point of view.

It is therefore crucially important not to fall prey to indicators-for-the-sake-of-indicators, nor to be tempted to use them in complete isolation from the array of other evaluative instruments available, which, although more evasive, have had a reasonable track record at guiding the learning of organizations. The graft onto the public policy process of a battery of performance indicators, and of a gross and imperfect monitoring protocol, without the complementary change in organizational culture to ensure that the appropriate degree of skepticism is attached to such indicators, will not produce a dramatic improvement in the process of social learning. Certainly, improvement does not automatically follow.

The crippling potentialities of quantophrenia

Quite clearly, the quantophrenic cosmology is quite reductive in its approach to the sort of inquiry reasonable public policy formation requires. Undoubtedly, there have been benefits derived from some of that work, yet we have no clear appreciation as to whether the quantophrenic experiments carried out over the last few decades have generated reasonable cost-benefit ratios.

The cynicism that has surrounded such discussion can best be captured by a crude comment made in yesteryears about PPBS – planning, programming, budgeting systems – the mother of all those quantophrenic experiments – launched in the 1960s in Canada (Balls 1970). The perplexing question in Ottawa in the early 1970s was – is it more PP or more BS? A less crude way to put this matter is that the general agreement in Ottawa (except among the operatives) was that the costs of this experiment had been greater than the benefits.

It would be nice if one could establish the necessary and sufficient conditions to ensure that the quantophrenic perspective would yield all the benefits attached to better marksmanship (for there are many) while avoiding the important distortion-generating impacts mentioned earlier. Unfortunately, such necessary and sufficient conditions cannot be defined. It is possible, however, to identify at least a few major sources of concern.

Uniformization in the face of pluralism and change

In a world that is pluralistic and continually evolving, one of the great dangers of formalization and quantification is the tendency for measures of central tendency to evolve into standards and norms that are applied across the board in the name of uniformity. These uniform standards have quite different impacts on differentiated publics, and tend to acquire a certain degree of non-negotiability over time. Indeed, it has been shown that such measures tend to foster centralization, and that such a propensity to impose uniformity does result in effectively Balkanizing the country (Migué 1994).

The uniformity frenzy, coupled with the egalitarian ideology (Kekes 2003), the folly of 'accountabilism' (Weinberger 2007), and the passion for transparency (Bennis 1976) amounts to a very toxic potion. Vibrant dynamic conservatism ensues, and extraordinary disinformation in arithmetical garb often sends citizens into catatonic states where common sense and the fundamental argument are easily lost.

Steering effects

The steering effects of perverse incentives have been noted earlier. The fixation on certain metrics to measure the performance of manpower agencies (number of job placements), or police forces (number of crimes resolved), and the like, has led such agencies to redirect their action away from difficult tasks (the placement of the long-term unemployed, or the effective resolution of crimes) into activities that would simply make the organization look good, according to the metrics in use: getting involved in routine hiring or the practice of plea bargaining with criminals to get them to admit to other crimes in exchange for reduced penalties. Metrics have often become powerful slogans (Schrage 2008).

Management Accountability Framework (MAF)
as an innocuous illustration

There is an incentive for those regulated, faced with such numerical targets that must be met in order to escape the censure of the regulators, to indulge in deception and lies when they realize that such numbers are often in the realm of the unverifiable.

In a recent series of breakfast meetings with executives of the federal public service (providing a safe space for discussion of taboo topics), I was not as astounded as some colleagues to hear about the world of MAF of the Treasury Board Secretariat.

Originally, the intention at the Treasury Board Secretariat was to gauge in a very rough way (1) whether the service providers were satisfied with their job, and (2) whether the citizen was satisfied with the service provided. It was felt that if both parties felt satisfied, then this was a fair indicator of quality.

However, once the quantophrenic brigade had hijacked this simple effort at providing a guesstimate, a framework was in place based on 10 interdependent expectations, 10 series of indicators meant to convey the breath and meaning of the expectations, and 10 series of measures meant to assess the progress toward the objectives described by the indicators. Responding to such requests has become a fairly demanding task, and the MAF scores have been used not only as a record of what is, but as a basis for evaluation and blaming, and to define what ought to be.

In a moment of candor, one participant confided that upon being chastised for having poorly 'maffed,' and being compared poorly with another department that had 'maffed' quite well, he felt quite astounded, since he had worked for years in the other department, and did not feel that they were performing that well. Upon subtle inquiry, it turned out that the other department had simply cooked up the numbers. And since the central bureau is flooded with such masses of numbers, it has no way to check, and the whole system becomes an invitation to deception.

The unintended costs of quantophrenia

It is difficult to measure the unintended costs of quantophrenia in the same manner that it is difficult to measure the unintended costs of the demoralization of the federal public service as a result of the 'Gomery' inquiry. Yet the fact that it is difficult to measure such costs precisely does not mean that they do not exist. The most important costs are obviously the result of a redirection of the efforts of the public service toward meeting artificial targets rather than doing their job with the maximum effectiveness, efficiency and economy, by making the highest and best use of their judgment and imagination. This leads to a form of reification of the burden of office, and to the development of ever more clever methods to generate good metrics, rather than doing a good job.

It is easy to gain a sense of the momentous amount of waste generated by enforcing the rituals focusing on formalizing and quantifying what has been in good currency for years, like personnel performance reviews. Samuel Culbert (2008) has suggested that one might usefully get rid of such perfunctory *performance reviews* and develop rather more iffy, and less easily quantifiable, *performance previews*, based on conversations designed to determine what an employee needs in order to be able to deliver what is expected of him or her.

Another important cost of the quantophrenic cosmology is the so-called Goodhart effect – a phenomenon akin to the Heisenberg principle, which suggests that quantifying transforms the world it tries to measure. Hoskin (1996: 265) has suggested a formulation of the Goodhart effect along the following lines: *every measure which becomes a target becomes a bad measure*. This is so because the calculative fantasies of managerialism transform the environment into which they are introduced. Individuals and organizations come to think of themselves as 'auditees,' and quantification distorts the character of the universe to which it is applied (Shore 2008): its effects are irreversible, and generate a fixation on the metric rather than on the creativity and initiative that any practice requires.

Getting results may be the explicit goal mentioned or pursued, but numerology transforms the very notion of what the goal is, of what the organization is about.

In order to engage stakeholders in action to eliminate or attenuate the malefits engendered by quantophrenia, it is not sufficient to denounce the quantophrenic perversion. An alternative cosmology must be provided, one less mesmerized and polluted by numbers. Otherwise, many stakeholders may not be willing to reconsider existing practices because they feel that some form of monitoring and performance-enhancement mechanism are necessary.

The ergonomics of the public policy process: focus on affordances

One alternative is building on the basic idea of ergonomics that "physical and cognitive affordances can help people to think about, know and use something more easily and to make fewer errors" (Rao and Sutton 2008: 132). These are concrete ways in which one draws attention to the problem to be solved, and provides easily learned and implemented tools that tend to generate a context that *affords 'action possibilities' and not others.*

The context has affordances that individuals and collectivities perceive, or learn to perceive. Learning to perceive affordances is a key kind of perceptual learning (Gibson 1982; Norman 1999). But "affordances are not fixed properties: they are relationships that hold between objects and agents ... to discover and make use of affordances is one of the important ways" to deal with novel situations (Norman 2007: 68-69). Learning to perceive affordances better, or developing ways to improve such perception, is the substance of social learning, and is at the core of innovation and innovative design.

Consequently, one can and should see the development of affordances as simple ways to lower the costs of thinking, to focus the mind and attention on key issues, to make sure that best practices and key ideas are communicated to neophytes in ways they can understand and apply.

A good example of an affordance is the checklist of things to verify used by pilots before taking off: an idea that would appear appallingly simplistic to policy makers or university professors. Yet, as Steven Tremain (quoted by Rao and Sutton 2008: 138) would say: would you board an airplane if the pilot were to be overheard saying, "I don't use checklists. I have been doing this for 20 years."

How many lives could be saved or policy failures avoided if the health care system and the public policy community were to emulate the aviation industry on this front. We already know the answer to this question from recent studies that have shown the extent to which such simple affordances as checklists in operating rooms have generated momentous improvements: "death rates fell overall by more than 40 percent and major complications by more than a third" (Priest 2009: A4).

The intent is not to provide a general ergonomics template for the public policy process *in toto*, which would be a futile effort. As Weick and Daft (1984) have shown in a classic article, such big and daunting problems are discouraging because they seem to pose insurmountable challenges. Consequently many are led to do nothing.

In fact, such big problems must be reframed as a series of smaller problems that can be tackled through concrete and manageable steps – issue domains and the like. Yet, one might still suggest a list of areas calling for the development of affordances in the different issue domains in public policy.

First, there is a need to name the issue of interest. *Naming* (as many activists know) has the great merit of making an issue more tangible, and to focus attention and energy on what the issue name has identified is of prime importance.

Second, *an enriched evidence-based exploration of the issues* grapples with the 'evidence,' wherever it is, and whatever form it might take, and is not restricting itself to hard material or quantophrenic evidence. It also takes into account intentionality, frames of reference, belief systems, and culture, to the full extent that these realities impact on the issue at hand.

Third, a refurbished mindset would put a premium on *the highest and best use of imagination, experimentalism and serious play* in the exploration of promising avenues for the design of viable responses to difficult situations. In that sense, it puts at the core of its inquiries an explicit social learning machine. The issue must not only be properly contextualized, but also subjected to a probing that attempts to make explicit the partiality of the frames used by the different stakeholders, in order to generate the requisite blending and blurring of frames that allow fruitful multilogues (Sabel 2001). This calls for a certain process of reconstruction: not only searching responses to the original questions, but wondering whether the original questions are the most useful ones, and exploring ways in which such questions might be modified, transformed and reframed.

At the core of experimentalism is prototyping. Prototyping means: (1) identifying some top requirements as quickly as possible; (2) putting in place a quick-and-dirty provisional medium of co-development; (3) allowing as many interested parties as possible to get involved as partners in designing a better arrangement; (4) encouraging iterative prototyping; and (5) thereby encouraging all the stakeholders, through playing with prototypes, to get a better understanding of the problems, of their priorities, and of themselves (Schrage 2000: 199ff). The purpose is to generate a creative interaction between people and prototypes. This may be even more important than creating a dialogue between people. It is predicated on a culture of active participation: a democratization of design and the sort of playfulness and adventure that is required for serious play with prototypes.

Fourth, this new mindset is meant to be *transformative*. It does not propose an exercise in hypothesis testing, but a commitment to entering a process of inquiry with a view to transforming the context that has led to the emergence of the thorny issue (Chait *et al.* 2005).

The traditional approaches, focused on attempts to falsify hypotheses about some objective reality, have generated too narrow a focus. For the social practitioner, what is central is an effort "to create a wholly new, unprecedented situation that, in its possibility for generating new knowledge, goes substantially beyond the initial hypothesis" (Friedman and Abonyi 1976: 938). This, in turn, calls for a different notion of 'success' or 'failure' that goes much beyond those in use in the usual physical, science-based process.

Conclusion

This chapter underlined the foot-binding effects of quantophrenia. It has tried to exorcise the futility of the quest for certainty through quantification, but it also has bemoaned a major loss ascribable to the quantophrenic frenzy: the loss of the centrality of experimentalism and social learning in most non-trivial aspects of public policy.

Far from being a panacea, quantification may be a bane, especially in the world of Kahneman and Tversky (1979), in which it has been shown that 'objective' results are elusive. When a slight change in the framing of a question, based on the same quantitative data, can generate very different responses, even from experts in the field, it is clear that the pretence of absolute illumination by quantification is untenable.

Consequently, unless auxiliary conditions are in place to ensure that the requisite social learning remains the main driving force, reification, distortion and mystification will ensue (Paquet 2009b).

My main message is simple: prudence is *de rigueur*.

A better way to summarize this message might be to borrow this phrase from Joseph Tussman, and suggest that it be inscribed at the top of the computer screen of all the would-be quantulators ... something that would remind them of the state of mind they have to maintain "... the state of mind of the magician who tremblingly invokes the powers he would use, knowing that if he gets the ceremony wrong what he invokes will destroy him. Neither romantic nor puritan, merely sensible ... " (Tussman 1989: 25).

References

Andreski, S. 1974. *Social Sciences as Sorcery*. Harmondsworth, UK: Penguin.

Balls, H.B. 1970. "New Techniques in Government Budgeting: Planning, Programming, and Budgeting in Canada," *Public Administration*, 48(3): 289-305.

Barnard, Chester. 1938. *The Functions of the Executive*. Cambridge, MA: Harvard University Press.

Becker, T.L. 1991. *Quantum Politics*. New York, NY: Praeger.

Bennis, W. 1976. "Have we gone overboard on the right to know?" *Saturday Review*, June 3, p. 18-21.

Bradwell, P. and R. Reeves. 2008. *Network Citizens*. London, UK: Demos.

Chait, R.P., W.P. Ryan and B.E. Taylor. 2005. *Governance as Leadership*. Hoboken, NJ: Wiley.

Cleveland, H. 2002. *Nobody in Charge*. San Francisco, CA: Jossey-Bass.

Culbert, S.A. 2008. "Get Rid of the Performance Review!" *Wall Street Journal*, October 20.

Durkheim, E. 1895/1988. *Les règles de la méthode sociologique*. Paris: Flammarion.

Friedmann, J. and G. Abonyi. 1976. "Social Learning: A Model for Policy Research," *Environment and Planning*, A(8): 927-940.

Fukuyama, F. 2004. *State-Building: Governance and World Order in the 21st Century*. Ithaca, NY: Cornell University Press.

Gallie, W.B. 1964. *Philosophy and the Historical Understanding*. London, UK: Chatto & Windus.

Gibson, J.J. 1982. "A Preliminary Description and Classification of Affordances" in E.S. Reed and R. Jones (eds.). *Reasons for Realism*. Hillsdale, NJ: Lawrence Erlbaum & Associates, p. 403-406.

Hoskin, K. 1996. "The 'awful idea of accountability': inscribing people into the measurement of objects" in R. Munro and J. Mouritsen (eds.). *Accountability – Power, Ethos and the Technologies of Managing*. London, UK: International Thompson Business Press, p. 265-282.

Hubbard, R. and G. Paquet. 2009. "Design Challenges for the Strategic State: Bricolage and Sabotage" in A.M. Maslove (ed.). *How Ottawa Spends 2009-10*. Montreal, QC and Kingston, ON: McGill-Queen's University Press, p. 89-114.

Kahneman, D. and A. Tversky. 1979. "Prospect Theory: An Analysis of Decision under Risk," *Econometrica*, XLVII, p. 263-291.

Kekes, J. 2003. *The Illusions of Egalitarianism*. Ithaca, NY: Cornell University Press.

McCarthy, H., P. Miller and P. Skidmore (eds.). 2004. *Network Logic*. London, UK: Demos.

Michael, D.N. 1993. "Governing by Learning: Boundaries, Myths and Metaphors," *Futures*, 25(1): 81-89.

Migué, J.L. 1994. "The Balkanization of the Canadian Economy: A Legacy of Federal Policy" in F. Palda (ed.). *Provincial Trade Wars: Why the Blockade Must End*. Vancouver, BC: Fraser Institute, p. 107-130.

Norman, D.A. 1999. "Affordances, Conventions and Design," *Interactions*, 6(3): 38-43.

Norman, D.A. 2007. *The Design of Future Things*. New York, NY: Basic Books.

Paquet, G. 1999. *Governance though Social Learning*. Ottawa, ON: University of Ottawa Press.

Paquet, G. 2005. *The New Geo-governance: A Baroque Approach*. Ottawa, ON: University of Ottawa Press.

Paquet, G. 2008a. *Gouvernance: mode d'emploi*. Montreal, QC: Liber.

Paquet, G. 2008b. "Governance as Stewardship," *www. optimumonline.ca*, 38(4): 14-27.

Paquet, G. 2009a. *Crippling Epistemologies and Governance Failures*. Ottawa, ON: University of Ottawa Press.

Paquet, G. 2009b. *Scheming virtuously: The road to collaborative governance*. Ottawa, ON: Invenire Books.

Parker, S. and N. Gallagher (eds.). 2007. *The Collaborative State*. London, UK: Demos.

Priest, L. 2009. "Simple checklists save lives in the operating room," *The Globe and Mail*, January 15, A4.

Rao, H. and R. Sutton. 2008. "The Ergonomics of Innovation," *The McKinsey Quarterly*, September 17.

Sabel, C.F. 2001. "A Quiet Revolution of Democratic Governance: Towards Democratic Experimentalism" in W. Michalski et al. (eds.). *Governance in the 21st Century*. Paris, FR: OECD, p. 121-148.

Schön, D.A. 1971. *Beyond the Stable State*. New York, NY: Norton.

Schrage, M. 2000. *Serious Play*. Boston, MA: Harvard Business School Press.

Schrage, M. 2008. "The Metric behind the Slogan," *Strategy & Business*, November 28, p. 1-3.

Shore, C. 2008. "Audit Culture and Illiberal Governance," *Anthropology Theory*, p. 278-298.

Simon, H.A. 1947. *Administrative Behavior*. New York, NY: Macmillan.

Smith, J.R. and C.A. Taylor. 1996. *Strengthening Policy Capacity*. Ottawa, ON: Canadian Centre for Management Development.

Sorokin, P.A. 1956. *Fads and Foibles in Modern Sociology and Related Sciences* Chicago, IL: Henry Regnery.

Spinosa, C. et al. 1997. *Disclosing New Worlds*. Cambridge, MA: MIT Press.

Sullivan, H. and C. Skelcher. 2002. *Working across Boundaries*. New York, NY: Palgrave Macmillan.

Taylor, C. 1997. "The ACIDD Test: a framework for policy planning and decision making," *Optimum*, 27(4): 53-62.

Treasury Board Secretariat (Canada). *TBS Management Accountability Framework*. http://www.tbs-sct.gc.ca/maf-crg/index-eng.asp [Accessed May 24, 2014].

Tussman, J. 1989. *The Burden of Office*. Vancouver, BC: Talonbooks.

Vickers, G. 1965. *The Art of Judgment*. London, UK: Chapman & Hall.

Weinberger, D. 2007. "The Folly of Accountabalism," *Harvard Business Review*, 85(2): 54.

Weick, K.E. and R.L. Daft. 1984. "Toward a model of organizations as interpretation systems," *The Academy of Management Review*, 9(2): 284-295.

CHAPTER 4

| On Disloyalty[1]

"Some circumstantial evidence is very strong,
as when you find a trout in the milk ..."
Henry David Thoreau

Introduction

This chapter examines the notion of disloyalty, and obliquely, the notion of dissent. It deconstructs the notion of disloyalty, the reasons why disloyalty is usually regarded as reprehensible, and through what mechanisms disloyalty might emerge. The first part of the chapter deals with these issues at a general level; the second portion focuses a bit more on the Canadian federal public service – a world in which this sort of issue is a matter of great consequence.

In passing, the paper also probes the virtue of dissent – not to be confused with disloyalty – and examines the realities of whistle-blowing and *affectio societatis*, and the myth of the state clergy – as interesting phenomena, illustrating the richness of the notion of disloyalty.

Loyalty and disloyalty as different nebulas

Some basic points

(1) The notion of loyalty is usually associated with the honouring of a moral contract, with living up to the

---

[1] Notes for a presentation to a seminar sponsored by the Institute of Public Administration of Canada (Toronto Chapter) on November 3, 2009.

legitimate expectations of those we are interacting with who have put their trust in us. Disloyalty is therefore a breach of trust.

Along the loyalty-disloyalty spectrum, those whose loyalty is *blind* give an absolute and transcendent value to this moral commitment. This is echoed in the motto – loyalty to country, right or wrong. They allow a particular commitment to take precedence over all others, and disallow any critical thinking to interfere with it. In this world of absolute loyalty, there is no possible questioning of loyalty to whom (a person), or to what (a cause), and no possibility of a review of such loyalties in the light of circumstances. Moreover, there is neither the possibility of certain loyalties acquiring different valences in certain circumstances over time, nor of the many loyalties requiring some difficult trade-offs. This is degree zero of critical thinking.

At the other end of the spectrum is *degree zero of loyalty*: this is the situation where any moral contract is totally contingent and revisable in view of evolving circumstances, as a result of benefit-cost analyses, or sheer whimsicality. In between these two positions lies a wide range of shades of loyalty or disloyalty: from the quasi-blind loyalty of public servants to their political masters (except in matters violating basic moral principles or the law), on the one hand, to disloyalty as an opportunistic self-serving choice, because the opportunity cost of loyalty is regarded as too high.

This one-dimensional characterization is a bit simplistic: the range from total other-directedness to total self-directedness is defined in connection with only one moral contract, and factors out the complexities of the multidimensional real world (a) where loyalties to person or cause are many, (b) where their intensity varies and evolves, (c) where trade-offs are constantly renegotiated depending on circumstances and values that are themselves evolving, and (d) where pluralism thrives (Kekes 1993).

In a more realistic view of the world, multiple moral contracts are nested in a network of heterarchical relationships, encompassing a variety of dimensions. According to circumstances that are ever-changing, and to levels of knowledge and competencies that are varied and imperfect, the legitimacies of the claims of the different parties to the moral contracts differ and evolve. In this world, the multiple loyalties may be starkly incompatible at any one time. In such a context, blind loyalty and chronic disloyalty *vis-à-vis* any other party on one particular issue (without some appreciation of the complexities of the situation and some critical thinking about the ordering or priorities of the different loyalties) are equally problematic. Moral pluralism prevails, so a balance of claims must be reached that allows no absolute overriding by any claim or value (*Ibid.*: 1993).

This balancing of claims is quite a daunting task. Critical thinking triggers negotiations leading to a decision about which loyalties will take precedence *hic et nunc*, and with what intensity, as a result of the definition of the relevant negotiated burden of office.

(2) The notion of burden of office refers to the duties that all officials are expected to accept as producers of governance. The burden of office is a nexus of moral contracts. Such officials are not necessarily rulers. Citizens who claim civil rights, like freedom of conscience, expression and association are officials of a sort, and are expected to accept duties as a counterpart in the moral contract that makes them producers of governance.

In a complex modern society, the citizen and all other officials have a multitude of relationships with the rest of society. They have a variety of interactions with other members of family, workplace, community of practice, polis,[2] etc., and each of these relations is defined more or less well by a moral contract spelling out the legitimate expectations of persons or groups with whom they interact. All citizens or officials are therefore embedded in an *n-dimensional* network

[2] Means city in Greek. It could also mean citizenship and body of citizens. http://en.wikipedia.org/wiki/Polis.

of relationships (Laurent and Paquet 1998). Corresponding to duties accepted (unconsciously, carelessly, unwittingly), there are rights more or less clearly agreed to that are provided to secure the required powers to perform these duties. In the case of persons or organizations that have accepted exceptional duties, there are usually corresponding exceptional rights or privileges.

Since most moral contracts are largely tacit, or ill-defined, or incomplete, and since their terms can be regarded as inherently contestable (i.e., reasonable persons may have different interpretations of them), there is much scope for disagreement and misunderstanding. This means that the benchmark by which loyalty or disloyalty may be gauged can be less clear than one would like and most often contestable.

The fact that the notion of burden of office is contestable and contested means that the notions of accountability (the nature of accounts to be rendered), of ethics (the nature of what is an acceptable and fair way to carry out one's burden of office in the view of other parties) and of loyalty/disloyalty (what can be reasonably and legitimately expected by and from other parties to the moral contract) are also of necessity contestable and contested.

The nature of the social armistices among the different loyalties, and the effective resolution of conflicts among them, are bound to evolve as a result of tensions that will lead to modifications in the terms of most or all of the underpinning moral contracts, and ultimately in the nature of the burdens of office. Therefore, it is quite difficult to pin down the notions of loyalty and disloyalty in the abstract.

The benchmark by which they can be gauged will vary in space and time, as the nature of the sort of armistices regarded as acceptable may vary. Moreover, it is unlikely that all parties at any one time or in any one locus will necessarily reach a consensus about a single interpretation. So the hope that a single guidepost can be used to arbitrate differences of opinion among parties on such matters is somewhat utopian, especially given the high degree of cognitive dissonance and the other mental prisons polluting such debates. The perspectives on these matters have not been quite the same either, depending on whether one deals with the notion of loyalty or disloyalty.

(3) The idea of a continuum from loyalty to disloyalty (like the idea of the continuum from trust to distrust) has proved less robust and helpful than anticipated. It is not unlike the evolution of H_2O as one proceeds up or down the Celsius scale: there are not only changes of degree along the way, but also changes of kind – from solid ice to liquid to gas as the temperature increases. Loyalty and disloyalty are, in fact, not the simple opposites or negatives one of the other, but they are realities that have been perceived as quite different in nature. As in the case of trust and distrust, it may be difficult to determine at exactly what point there is a change of kind, but it definitely occurs (Hardin 2004).

For instance, loyalty is a very 'thin' concept: one can be loyal to anything and anyone, and indeed may be loyal without knowing it, and even without any idea of what loyalty is. It connotes perseverance in meeting the expectations built into a relationship. Most often, loyalty connotes an unquestioning, indiscriminating and undiscerning force: "loyalty is a dog without moral judgment" (Tussman 1989: 66) – that is, as we mentioned earlier, some sort of degree zero of critical thinking.

Disloyalty is a very much 'thicker' concept. It "is more of a moral, social, public or institutional phenomenon, requiring more in the way of context. Before we can have disloyalty, we need a setting sufficiently rich to give rise to normative expectations" (Keller 2007: 213). Moreover, most of the time there is a much higher degree of deliberateness in disloyalty than in loyalty.

Neither loyalty nor disloyalty is of necessity enlightened – it may be self-serving, and may threaten the social order. But loyalty has acquired the garment of a virtue in many circles while disloyalty is most often regarded as a vice.

Shades of disloyalty

The 'thick' nature of the notion of disloyalty makes the context and burden of office immensely important. Since (as was mentioned earlier) disloyalty needs a setting sufficiently rich to give rise to strong normative expectations, it is difficult to ascertain disloyalty without a fair understanding of the nature of the issues involved. So this cannot be a discussion conducted in general, but rather at the level of particular issue domains.

Two important dimensions of the context are worth exploring in a preliminary way: the difference between convergent and divergent issues, and a sense of what the notion of issue domains might mean in a concrete way.

(1) One of the important sources of the growing degree of dissensus among officials (citizens and all other officials) is obviously the greater complexity of current policy issues, the hyper-turbulence and uncertainty of the external environment, and the greater degree of pluralism of the texture of society. But the growing acuteness of these differences of opinion may also be due to the fact that issues under discussion only rarely raise *convergent problems* these days (for which the multiplicity of diverse responses offered tend cumulatively and gradually through time to converge toward an agreed-upon response or consensus), but rather *divergent problems* (for which, *a contrario*, the more the problem is clarified, the more divergent and irreconcilable the points of view become).

Fritz Schumacher (1977: ch. 10), who proposed this distinction, used education as a fair example of an issue raising a clutch of divergent problems – indeed, the more one delves into what would be necessary to better raise and educate a child, the more complex and intractable the problem becomes. This is why Freud used to say that to govern, to cure, and to educate are "impossible professions" (Innerarity 2002: 193).

In the face of divergent problems, there is an ever greater possibility of different stakeholders reasonably defending incompatible approaches, and therefore more scope for dissent and for the possibility of disloyalty of one sort or another. In the many-dimensional world of governance (Paquet 2008) where 360-degree loyalties are likely to be difficult if not impossible to reconcile, divergent problems are the rule.

(2) Disloyalty as a breach of trust depends on the intensity of the normative expectations: the greater the intensity of the legitimate normative expectations, the more egregious the breach of trust and the more reprehensible the disloyalty.

In any governance context (where governance is defined as effective coordination when power, resources and information are widely distributed), different sorts of accountabilities are a useful gauge of the normative expectations attached to the burden of office: ethical relations are the flip side of these accountabilities. Disloyalties might therefore be categorized according to the valence and intensity of the accountability/ ethical relations, and to the depth of the trust violated when there is a breach of trust.

De-squishing the concept of trust is therefore crucial to an understanding of disloyalty. But trust is domain-specific – you would not trust your dentist to repair your car (Keen 1998)! Therefore, disloyalty has to be dealt with at the issue domain level: one is not disloyal in general, but disloyal with reference to normative expectations in a given issue domain, as defined by the burden of office, and as gauged by the community of practice. Without specifications, the sort of trust that is betrayed is rather difficult to define.

The more convergent the problem, and the more fully integrated and mature the community of practice, the sharper is the definition of the burden of office, and the easier it is to identify disloyalty. The more divergent the problem, and the more diffuse and anomic the community of practice, the fuzzier is the burden of office, and the more difficult it will be to identify disloyalty. Hard and soft disloyalties ensue.

Setting and source of our hypothesis

The emergence of the hypothesis of the existence and increase of disloyalty in the Canadian federal public service took shape in discussions with senior public servants at an APEX seminar on February 28, 2007 (Hubbard and Paquet 2007). From the very start, these officials declared emphatically that they felt loyal. This was a matter of both personal comfort and pride, but without being very specific about either their burden of office or about the norms they felt had to be honoured to ensure loyalty.

This is not surprising since the public servants' burden of office is built on many unwritten (even un-stated and ill-understood) clauses defining the understandings and expectations of others – bosses, peers, co-workers, clients, possibly subordinates and/or partners – with whom they collaborate. In the simplest of terms, disloyalty means breaking any such moral contract deliberately and knowingly.

Yet as the discussions progressed, almost all participants recalled and described instances of disloyalty they had observed, and they reluctantly came to the conclusion that disloyalty would appear to have increased. The reasons mentioned to explain such phenomena were that their group had been experiencing a dual series of shocks over the last decade or two.

(1) The first series of shocks occurred in the 1980s and 1990s. These shocks have been well documented (Paquet and Pigeon 2000; Paquet 2009a: 179ff) and came to challenge the public service culture as it stood, *circa* the 1980s: permanent employees, appointed on the basis of merit, a job-description, generous fringe benefits, job security and a career-path, expectations of anonymity, impartiality and accountability to ministers.

In the 1980s, this traditional culture was challenged *from within* in a rather timid way by Public Service 2000. It pointed to the need for public employees to attend more closely to the needs of the citizens, and to make the highest and best use of their creativity in their work. There was also a need for the employer to improve training, development, and career planning, and to develop a new focus on accountability as responsibilities were devolved to managers so that they could manage. However, this challenge did not shake the traditional culture in a fundamental way.

It was only in the 1990s, as a result of the fiscal crisis, that the culture was hit by strong pressure *from without*. While it is difficult to clearly establish the exact moment of the hit, the message was first starkly presented in the Directors of Personnel discussion paper in the fall of 1994. This document, explicitly inspired by David Noer's *Healing the Wounds* (1993), set out to "define the steps required to achieve a new public service model for Canada" (Directors of Personnel 1994: 2).

Noer's message was simple: (1) to acquire the new required flexibility, the old employment contract that guaranteed much security to the employee needed to be abrogated; (2) the traditional employment contract might not have been very healthy in any case, for it fostered an undesirable sort of co-dependency between employees and their organization.

The Directors of Personnel discussion paper was even starker: it diagnosed the traditional employment contract as "unrealistic," "not necessary or affordable," and "an unhealthy expectation" (*Ibid.*: 5). The document suggested the termination of the then current policy of conversion from term to indeterminate employment after five years; it put forward a framework where "employees not the employer, are responsible for their own employment options, but the employer would provide support to enable the continued employability of staff" (*Ibid.*: 17). The document also stated that the "moral framework" (*Ibid.*: 9) had to be renegotiated.

In May 1995, the President of the Public Service Commission, Ruth Hubbard, sketched a three-tiered-system model of the public service as it might emerge, with a small "core of permanent and highly-skilled knowledge workers, supported by a pool of short-term employees who work in government for stints of several months or years and move on … (plus) a "para-public service that could emerge as various levels of government cooperate on delivering services and as private-public partnerships take over services that were once provided by government" (Hubbard 1995). While the contours of the new employment contract(s) Hubbard had in mind remained vague, the strategic direction hinted at was congruent with the contents of the Directors of Personnel document.

Donald Savoie (2003) could say that the deal that ensured that bureaucratic officials would provide the government of the day with "non-partisanship, loyalty, impartiality, discretion and professionalism, in return for anonymity and security of tenure" (*Ibid.*: 17) had all but disappeared.

(2) The second series of shocks came as a result of the more recent switch in government regime – from majority to minority, and from Liberal to Conservative – that has exacerbated the strains as bureaucrats came to be expected to shift their loyalty to the agenda and policies of the new (and yet maybe temporary) government, and to serve it creatively and loyally. When one political party has held power for 10 or 15 years, many of the old ways come to be regarded as 'normal and preferred' by public servants hired, promoted, and engaged by that government. Moreover, when the new government is a minority government that could be soon toppled, the urge to shift one's involvement and engagement might be considerably slowed down and attenuated.

Faced with having to forge new direct and indirect relationships that called for the acceptance of perspectives very different from those they were used to, public servants had two choices – leaving ('exiting' physically, or hibernating by leaving their souls at home and focusing on fulfilling only a modicum of technical duties) or trying to propose modifications ('voice' alternative views, and propose alternative ways to define and implement what the new government has in mind). Some have suggested that a measure of loyalty to the organization/institution may be how long one uses 'voice' before 'exiting,' or beginning to indulge in disloyal behaviour passively or actively. The latter point underlines the clear distinction between open dissent and disloyalty: passive assent (e.g., reluctance to raise meaningful questions in a positive way; tardiness in questioning when questioning is warranted; silence when innovative ways of handling contentious issues are thinkable and available) is often an instance of disloyalty.

It is hardly surprising that the broken bargain of the 1990s (that had already generated a great cooling-off in the relationships between politicians and bureaucrats, and a certain circling of the wagons by bureaucrats intent on protecting their privileges and on using all the means at their disposition to immunize themselves from the fate promised by the planned new bargain), and the new strains added to the politico-bureaucratic relations by the shift to a minority/Conservative government (sharpening the cleavage between a segment of the bureaucracy and the politicians) have generated understandable tensions. These could only be expected to lead to increased disaffection, and consequently to a lesser engagement, a tendency to re-affirm ever more strongly the legitimacy of their expertise as opposed to the dubious legitimacy of those churned out by the democratic election process, and, as might be expected, forms of passive and active disloyalty.

Such at least is the hypothesis that has emerged from preliminary interviews and discussions with senior federal public servants.

Is disloyalty increasing?

Disloyalty entails some disagreement leading to a misalignment between the direction chosen by the principal (the government in power) and the direction followed by agents (the senior bureaucrats). This disagreement and misalignment can have many sources and take many forms. For instance, it may simply be ascribable to miscommunication, or to poor motivation, or to a lack of effort, but it may also be due to deliberate sabotage. It would be silly, however, to reduce the notion of disloyalty to the sole activity of active sabotage. On the other hand, it might be excessive to ascribe to disloyalty what might be better explained by forms of free-riding and laziness. Or would it be?

Consequently, a portion of what has been called X-inefficiency (Leibenstein 1976, 1987) is clearly ascribable to casual organizational slack, but some of it may well be ascribed to lack of motivation and effort, due to resentment and disloyalty to the organization.

One very important source of friction has to do with sharp differences of opinion as to who is authorized to define the public interest: the elected officials, or the unelected public servants who may believe that they know more (because they are experts) and may claim to have a better appreciation of what is best for the country than the elected representatives.

The dominium of democratic values (if it is so agreed) dictates what must happen when there is dissent between politicians and bureaucrats on the matter of what is in the public interest. The bureaucrats must use their 'voice' to bring the full force of persuasion, based on their expertise, to get the political authorities to modify their views. In the discussion, the bureaucrats may discover that there is no possible meeting of minds, or they may discover that new imaginative ways of stating the problem may generate creative compromises that satisfy both parties. Depending on the criticality of the issue, if there is no possible reconciliation of the different points of view, the bureaucrat may either choose to resign or agree to creatively help the politician to carry out the policy of choice in as an effective a way as possible, despite his/her reservations.

The behaviour of one deputy minister who chose to leave because he was unable/unwilling to support the new government's approach, or another who chose, instead, to "put words in the mouth of his unsuspecting minister in the other official language – a language he did not quite master …" were evoked in the 2007 discussions with senior executives. Participants agreed that the first was acting with integrity, while the second was being disloyal.

The rise in disloyalty may not depend solely on the circumstances as defined by the narrow context. Federal public servants do not live in isolation from the broader society, and the broad context may have an impact on the coefficient of loyalty in good currency in a society that has a reverberation effect on particular issue domains. William Safire (1994) has denounced what he has called the rise of a "new disloyalty" – a pernicious worldwide devaluation of loyalty that has permeated the workplace everywhere. Such forces, one would expect, have affected the workplace at the federal public service level as well, and generated some disloyalty. In that sense, the public sector is no different from the private sector in Canada, where polling data would appear to support strongly the hypothesis of rising workplace disloyalty (Rynor 2009).

Finally, the very wide range of definitions of the phenomena covered by the notion of *disloyalty* – not only passive and active disloyalty, but the whole more difficult terrain of lessening engagement and commitment, of 'hibernation,' of a systematic dwarfing of the notion of burden of office, of an erosion of the sense that democratic values must prevail on so-called expertise, etc. – has made it easier to arrive at a consensus on the general fact that disloyalty is growing.

But there has been sharp disagreement about the form this growing disloyalty has taken. Insiders who were interviewed felt that active sabotage has always been limited in the federal public service, and has probably not increased significantly over the last decade. But most felt that the rest of the disloyalty nebula had increased.

In fact, the cautious conclusion of our 2007 discussions was that one could observe a growing *culture of disloyalty* enveloping the public service today, as a result of the whole array of forces mentioned above. This may be perceived as rather weak anecdotal evidence from interviews and discussions with a few dozen senior executives. Yet the result of these discussions and interviews is no weaker than most of what is found in the traditional public administration literature – passing references to anonymous interviews having been conducted.

Disloyalty as akin to the underground economy phenomenon

Understandably, there has been much vibrant denial by Canadian federal public service senior officials, when confronted with the airing of these conjectures.

I was reminded of the impact of a paper I wrote some 25 years ago (Paquet 1989) on the size of the underground economy in Canada, and on the consequent loss of tax revenue to governments. I was speculating in that paper (on the basis of anecdotal evidence, but also on the basis of a full decade of observations as an economic journalist) that the size of the underground economy was immensely greater than was acknowledged by Statistics Canada, and that it was growing fast. It earned me a free lunch and a stern dressing down from a high official of Statistics Canada, demanding a righting of my ways and an end to my dangerous ruminations that could only be interpreted as suggesting that our national statistical agency was missing a big chunk of what was going on in the country.

Many guesstimates of the size of the Canadian underground economy (and of the consequent size of the loss of tax revenue) were provided in the following decade – all equally large, equally based on oblique measures, and equally quickly dismissed. One of the more recent studies by Giles and Tedds (2002) made use of more formidable econometric tools, and brought them to bear on the still quite fuzzy reality of the underground economy. These results (still based on oblique gauges) suggested that the underground economy had grown from 3.5 percent of GDP in 1976 to 16 percent in 1995, and that the yearly loss of tax revenue had grown from some \$2 billion in 1976 to \$44 billion in 1995. One can easily imagine that these numbers have reached new heights in 2014.

Earlier guesstimates had been merrily rejected (cognitive dissonance galore!) on the basis of some ready dismissal of the evidentiary base as not meeting the standards of evidence of the national agency. The same argument has been used to dismiss this more sophisticated study just as merrily. The denial persists, and no serious policy action has been initiated to deal with the problem.

The difficulty in gaining an exact quantitative measure of disloyalty is not unlike the difficulty of gauging the size of the underground economy. But this does not mean that, because it cannot be measured precisely, it does not exist – even though such claim is routinely made in quantophrenic policy circles.

To generate greater attention to these provisional soft conjectures about the rise in disloyalty, it might be useful to throw some light on the mechanisms underpinning such a drift toward disloyalty.

Analytical framework

In this section, I suggest a provisional map of the forces and mechanisms at work in generating disloyalty, in the hope that it might help to unearth additional oblique evidence that might suggest that these mechanisms have indeed been at work.

At the core of the framework, there are three mechanisms:
- *mechanism I* – the way a self-interested satisficer takes into account perceived social rewards and penalties generated by the context when deciding how to behave (Jones 1984);
- *mechanism II* – the way experiences with changes in the context lead to value change and act as loyalty filtres – i.e., experiences redirecting loyalties (Mesthene 1970; Akerlof 1984); and
- *mechanism III* – the way the impact of the reshuffling of loyalties is dramatically modified by the existence of exit/ voice costs and opportunities, and by group reactions to loyalty and disloyalty (Hirschman 1970; Levine and Moreland 2002).

These mechanisms underpin a plausible stylized tale that might be presented in the following way.

First, individuals make choices (on the basis of limited information and limited rationality), taking into account not only personal rewards and penalties, but also perceived social rewards and penalties. The social context generating such perceived social rewards and penalties depends a great deal on custom, tradition and *ethos* pertaining to organizations and issue domains, and tends to generate what Cass Sunstein (2003) calls *collective conformism* – a tendency to stick to established patterns, even as group members change. This is the compounding effects of the environmental *ethos* and the organizational culture.

Second, shocks from both within and without, from time to time, generate changes in both the environmental *ethos* and organizational culture (like changes in technology), and these modify the choice options over time. Therefore, choice behaviour changes, and changed choice behaviour (with appropriate lags) becomes conceptualized and habitualized as change in values. As individuals or groups experience some such transformation, it acts as a *loyalty filtre* that may change the mix of personal self-interest and group interest that influences choice behaviour. This may act in either direction: either by increasing loyalty to self or group or tribe or institution, or by diminishing it.

Third, the impact of the change in the mix of loyalties may, in turn trigger the decision to exit the organization or concern, or to make more use of the voice option to get the organization to modify the tradition or the covenant that members are asked to conform to. Depending on the ease and cost of exit, the effectiveness of voice, and the dynamics of group reaction to such actions, the pressure on the organization to modify the tradition will either decrease (as non-conformists leave) or increase (as the voice option generates an emergent activist public). In the process, agents who may choose not to exit because the costs are too high, and not to exercise the voice pressure for creative reform (because again the costs are too high, and the probability of success too low), may displace their main loyalty away from what their burden of office might dictate toward the 'tribe' or sub-groups they identify with, and become passively or actively disloyal to the organization and institution.

These three mechanisms act in a loop.

Let us assume, for illustration purposes, the following stylized hypothetical situation at the bureaucratic-political interface:

(1) a dire global economic situation entailing a high cost of exit (because of lack of equally satisfactory work conditions elsewhere);

(2) the breaking of the traditional political-bureaucratic bargain; and

(3) a new (and quite different) minority government following years of dominance by another political party – with the consequence that the effectiveness of the voice option may be limited (either because the bureaucracy is shackled by mental prisons inherited from the past that are not in line with the philosophy of the new government, or because of the diffidence of the new government in the face of a bureaucracy they have not got full confidence in).

It might be conjectured that (the bargain being broken and both the exit and voice options blocked) the disloyalty of the senior bureaucrats may increase through the operations of a loyalty filtre that re-enforces the loyalty to the well-protected tribe of senior bureaucratic officials, as opposed to the loyalty to the elected government and its institutions, as the burden of office would dictate. The result is active and passive disloyalty.

One might also conjecture that the disloyalty will materialize with different intensity in different issue domains, depending on (1) whether the problems are divergent or convergent; (2) the sharpness of the cleavages between older and newer views in different issue domains; (3) the particularities of the senior officials and politicians in place; and (4) the costs of exit and voice options in these domains.

For instance, in issue domains where the new government's decentralization drive and its propensity to reduce state-centricity are likely to be most disturbing to the existing order, one would expect a much higher degree of disloyalty. In the same spirit, one would expect senior officials fully engrossed by the principles of the last government on these fronts to be more aggressively disloyal than those who are more operations-and-efficiency-driven.[3]

None of this will materialize brusquely and overnight.

One should keep in mind that, in the case of the federal public service, the long tradition of the loyalty of the bureaucracy to the elected government (until the breaking of the traditional bargain), and the large portion of governmental operations where contentious/divergent issues like those mentioned above are not prominent, would lead to a conjecture that the percentage of aggressively disloyal senior public servants is not very large. However, to the extent that perceived explicit disloyalty is not punished (but rewarded, by international postings for example), and that disloyal senior bureaucrats are not clearly identified or identifiable (therefore, one does not easily know who is disloyal), even as small a percentage as five percent of senior officials being disloyal is of consequence. It most certainly would suffice to generate a climate of paranoia in the whole system, to entice the political branches to react negatively, and to dramatically corrupt the bureaucratic-political interface.

Disloyalty is growing: some conjectures

Certain observations would appear to indicate that the three mechanisms mentioned above are at work, and such observations provide a plausible explanation for the pattern of behaviour conjectured. In order to make the point, allow me to focus mainly on the bureaucratic-political interface for senior officials in the Canadian federal public sector.

Some things to keep in mind

The experience of Paul Tellier in the 1980s appears to reveal that the loyalty of senior officials could then be carried from one majority government to the next. Tellier was clearly associated with the Liberal Party (in what appeared to be a more partisan way than is usual) and yet became the Clerk of Privy Council for the Mulroney (Progressive Conservative) government that took power immediately afterward.

[3] For a cautionary tale about this sort of phenomenon, see Paquet 2013a.

Effective loyalty filtres emerged in the 1990s. First in line was the El-Mashat affair in May-June 1991, where a comedy of errors led to the embarrassment of the Mulroney government, and to the indictment of senior bureaucrats for lack of due diligence and lack of professionalism. Then came the mid-1990s and the traumatic edicts discussed above in the wake of the fiscal crisis: the famous discussion paper, *The Way Ahead for the Public Service*, in the fall of 1994, that concluded that a career public service is no longer "necessary or affordable"; the 1994-95 Annual Report of the Public Service Commission stating as a **fact** "that the implicit employment contract which guaranteed relative job security to employees has been abrogated": and Program Review with its adjuvant frozen compensation, etc. (Linquist and Paquet 2000; Paquet and Pigeon 2000). Massive reduction in personnel, a salary freeze, and scaling down in work conditions across the board took their toll. But the economy was thriving at the time, exit was not unduly costly, so many of the disgruntled took their leave and those left behind appeared again to have served the government well.

Something dramatically different occurred in the last quinquennium of the first decade of the new century.

First, Prime Minister Harper was seen as arriving on the stage with a mindset quite different from the one dominating the scene earlier. His minority governments generated apprehension in many senior officials, but also a sense that they might not have to change their mindset too fast since this government might not be there long.

Second, there has always been a protective belt around senior officials – they take care of their own – but this corporatism has become much more robust of late as the 'tribe' or the 'system' came to regard itself as under threat. Both a greater sense of entitlement and a greater sense of self-preservation appear to have developed in the tribe of senior officials. The Gomery inquiry has provided ample evidence of the new capacity for senior officials to 'take care of their own.'

Third, moral relativism reached new heights in the last decade in Canada and elsewhere, so the sense of entitlement at the highest levels of the Canadian federal public service have no doubt also increased dramatically. This should not be lightly generalized (and it must be emphasized that there is still a vast majority of senior officials totally devoted to the public good), but the famous line "I am entitled to my entitlements" (à la David Dingwall), or the abuses allowed to prevail unchecked for the longest time (à la Radwinski), or the closed and seemingly impermeable culture of the RCMP, etc., are echoes of some erosion of the moral foundations on which the public service was built, and of the formation of enclaves or self-referential tribes in the Canadian federal public service (Paquet 2007).

Mechanisms at work

By looking at the three mechanisms mentioned above in action, it is possible to detect subtle and yet significant changes that might hold clues about their operations being the source of increased disloyalty. The objective of this portion of the paper is to invite the reader to probe the learning loop in search of either positive or negative support for the general hypothesis presented earlier: the work of loyalty filtres, the deflection of the impact of the new mix of loyalties toward disloyalty, and the development of a new conformism of disloyalty. Some illustrative points are made below re: the mechanisms II, III, and I.

(1) the Mesthene-Akerlof Type II mechanisms

Part of the shuffling of loyalties from the institution to personal and tribe priorities has been the result of a strong appreciation of the relative importance of expertise, while democratic values and representative democracy have suffered some devaluation. This had been slowly developing since the 1970s, but never more so than in the recent past when credentialism appeared to have come to trump all other sources of legitimacies.

This has most certainly dramatically influenced hiring and promotion and, as a result, accelerated the shift from institutional/organizational loyalty to group/tribe/profession loyalty: as the status of elected officials got downgraded, and the expertise of the bureaucracy was lionized, their relative influence on governance changed accordingly. Tribe in some cases has meant profession, but in the case of the very senior public servants, it has become the 'community of senior officials.'

Slipping from a role of advisor to the politicians into the role of managing them and arrogating the decision-making process to oneself is a very short step. The managerial class has obviously not hijacked the political process, but it has claimed an ever greater place at the decision-making table, and often served the government less than perfectly (Hubbard and Paquet 2009).

(2) the Levine-Moreland-Hirschman Type III mechanisms
The new mix of loyalties may take many forms, depending on context and circumstances. The compounding of: (1) a sharp cleavage between the old and new policy directions; (2) an emerging sense in the tribe of senior federal bureaucrats that they are better interpreters of the public interest than elected officials; (3) the perceived temporariness of the minority governments; (4) the limited exit possibilities for senior bureaucrats in difficult economic times; and (5) the great tolerance for disloyalty to politicians by the top layer of the bureaucracy but also by opinion moulders like columnists and other *magistrats de l'immédiat* – have generated a significant erosion of the notion of burden of office.

A meaningful minority of senior middle-aged officials may have, therefore, found themselves unable to serve the government loyally, and are yet unable to find an exit leading to an equally cushy job. This opened the gate to disloyalty (passive or active), depending on the nature of the cleavages (actively in agonistic issues, passively in less agonistic files, and by hibernation in other files), depending on the protection of the tribe, and on temperaments.

To the extent that group loyalties have grown significantly, and that paranoia has developed between the politicians and the bureaucrats, a quasi-psychosis has developed that has persuaded many bureaucrats that the government is not interested in listening to their voices. The media frenzy, especially through opinion-moulding columnists, has contributed significantly to this deterioration by generating a whole folklore of half-truths that have served disgruntled bureaucrats well in rationalizing their soft disloyalties.

(3) the Jones Type I mechanisms

Two factors might be worth underlining in the recent development of the broad social forces that have influenced choice behaviour and loyalties, and impacted on the *ethos* and the organizational culture of the Canadian public service.

The evidence of moral relativism is quite widely spread. The paraphernalia of underlying social values carried by religion, family and community are no longer in good currency. Even the very notion of public service has been redefined by the public choice literature as simply fuelled by self-interest.

So one should not be surprised that the internalization of such a value system has led a significant number of public servants to allow their own personal interests, or the interests of the tribe, to take precedence over what the tradition and custom of serving the public may have meant in the past. This is the new conformism.

The second point that has been less fully acknowledged is the growth of sub-group or tribal identity.

We know that, with the decline of grand narratives in general, agents have turned more and more toward their community of practice as the relevant unit to which they have loyalty. This has been recognized in different work milieus, but it has become a feature of the federal public service at all levels over the last while. One might underline, in particular, the growth of the 'community of regulators' and other similar communities that clutches of federal public servants have come to regard as their main or principal anchor within the public service. Such enclaves have come to generate the recognized reference points and standards of behaviour – particular organizational cultures – where corporatist tribal/professional sentiments trump democratic engagement.

(4) cumulative causation toward the neurotic State

Each element in the learning loop integrating these three mechanisms, however limited in scope, has a multiplier effect through that loop. The permission to be disloyal, and the rationalization of such disloyal action as work done in the *intérêts supérieurs de la nation*, can only snowball and generate some additional paranoia on the part of the elected officials. Such paranoia can then be used to rationalize further disloyalty since it has been argued openly that the government in place does not echo 'fundamental Canadian values.' This is a pattern that could be observed even in the 1990s (Juillet and Paquet 2002), but the recent heightened tensions have obviously accelerated the process.

This state of affairs has already reached a critical level in many democracies, and certain countries have recognized it. The United Kingdom recently felt it necessary to use a *Magna-Carta*-type mechanism, and approved a formal code enforced by the highest authorities on both sides – the Prime Minister and the Civil Service Commission – (i) requiring ministers to respect the impartiality of the public service, and to give fair weight to their advice; and (ii) requiring the civil service to set out the facts and relevant issues truthfully, and to correct any errors as soon as possible, and not knowingly mislead ministers, Parliament, or others (Thomas 2009: 51). This was a vibrant re-assertion of democratic values in circumstances where they are losing their dominium.

One may legitimately wonder whether the present Canadian insouciance on this front (about the failings on both sides of the political-bureaucratic equation) is the result of much naïvety, immense cognitive dissonance, reprehensible disingenuity, or worse (Hubbard and Paquet 2010: conclusion).

In praise of anecdotal evidence

Many may grant some general plausibility to my argument but bemoan that before taking action better evidence is needed. In a world that has become mesmerized by scientistic quantophrenic arguments, there seems to be little place left for the force of practical intelligence and judgment. Yet our daily life is fully inhabited by the use of rules of thumb, and the uses of gut feelings are at the basis of our survival. Medical doctors and a multiplicity of professionals (including professional baseball or hockey players) take action not on the basis of computation, but on the basis of a practical intelligence that enables them to amass a large amount of scattered information, and to form a plausible judgment that they would often find difficult to explain in detail, or to translate into a protocol or an algorithm (Gladwell 2005; Gigerenzer 2007).

If strategists or designers waited until all their interventions had been scientifically vindicated by double-blind testing, there is much that would never get done. Most often, they are in the position of a backwoods mechanic, who does not have all spare parts available to him and must be satisfied with vicarious functioning to get the vehicle back on the road (Gigerenzer 2001).

In human affairs, especially in the world of strategy, the information is never completely available and certain. One must act on the basis of imperfect and incomplete information; otherwise, much damage may ensue. Scientism and the cult of quantophrenia can become crippling epistemologies and the source of many a governance failure (Paquet 2013b).

What a practical mindset would suggest is that one must grapple with 'evidence' wherever it is and whatever form it might take. It cannot rely on hard quantophrenic material evidence alone, but must take into account all the realities that have an impact on the issue at hand, and even put a premium on the best use of imagination and foresight in exploring what is in the process of emerging. It is the only way to be *ecologically rational* (i.e., taking action that takes into account all the cues from the environment, and fits with what the environment calls for) (Paquet 2009b).

Evidence and cues exist at the present time about the existence and rising level of disloyalty. By itself, this does not give any certitude about the source of the problem or the potential cures. But it establishes that the problem is not *un être de raison*. The current trend toward disengagement has been recorded by longitudinal federal public service surveys. They have noted a significant increase in the rationale for wanting to leave the public service as something due to conflict between personal and organizational values. The registered higher level of disengagement of late has been significant enough to generate some action at the Privy Coucil Office level. The fact that even the PCO is concerned may not persuade radical skeptics that disloyalty is on the rise, but given the congenital cognitive dissonance of the PCO, it must mean that their intelligence corroborates the sort of ethnographic material collected by interviews (like the ones Hubbard and I collected) and it lends some support to my hypothesis.

In particular, the evidence of a shift in loyalty from democratic values to the interests of the community of practice is a matter of great consequence. It has been clearly perceived by astute observers of the Ottawa scene like Hugh Segal that, as he put it, "the federal public service is about the federal administration first, its institutions, prerogatives, etc., ... and their protection" (Segal 2010: 99). Any political ethnographer familiar with the Ottawa scene knows it well. Yet it is only very rarely that one can observe in official documents a sleight of hand that indicates that the tribe is willing to take action to serve the tribe to the detriment of the citizenry. This has been the case in the debauching of the mandate of Service Canada (Hubbard and Paquet 2009).

Most of the time, it is not only difficult, but quite delicate and perilous to expose disloyalty in Ottawa. The tribe can hit back with a vengeance. I can still remember the personal costs borne by Scott Gordon as a result of his exposé of James Coyne's misdeeds some 50 years ago. This is a cautionary tale. Gordon's original letter denouncing Coyne was signed by 29 economists, and the short book (Gordon 1961) he wrote soon after demonstrated very effectively that there had been deception on the part of the Governor of the Bank of Canada. Indeed, Coyne was fired as Governor of the Bank of Canada by the Canadian government soon afterward.

But after this event, Gordon was marginalized and shunned by the federal bureaucracy. His part-time career as a mediator in public service affairs was brought to a halt, and he was explicitly ignored by a royal commission later struck on monetary affairs (even though he was one of the best known Canadian experts in this area). He was later to depart from Canada to pursue a most successful academic career in the United States. This cautionary tale illustrates the perils of exposing deception and misinformation generated by officialdom in the federal public sector in Canada.

A recent incident brought to my attention may allow the reader to reflect for a moment on the extent to which what is denounced here has permeated the bureaucratic practice. It pertains to the explicit corporatist refusal by a cadre of federal public servants posted abroad to carry out intelligence work and to provide advice to the government on whether or not Canada should take action to intervene on behalf of Canadians embroiled in difficulties with the judiciary in foreign countries. The Canadian government wanted Canadian officials *in situ* to provide intelligence about the legitimacy and reliability of the judiciary system in question and the exact circumstances of the case before deciding on what course of action would appear to be warranted. This cadre of federal public servants stated that they felt it was not their responsibility to do so, that it was in violation of Canadian values as they understood them, and that their role was to defend Canadians unconditionally. They felt that it was not their job to supply information to the government on the advisability of providing help (or not), and of what sort, in particular situations.

In the face of such evidence, it would be *insouciance déréglée ou téméraire* (the definition of criminal negligence in the Criminal Code) not to pay attention.

Four clarifying vignettes

The fact that there is no incontrovertible quantitative evidence of increased demonstrated disloyalty should not lead us to ignore the rampant toxic phenomenon, but it should not lead to overstating the case irresponsibly, either.

The following vignettes are designed to sharpen somewhat the focus of a needed inquiry into this phenomenon of increasing disloyalty and decreasing trust by looking at four epiphenomena that might help give a better sense of the different forms distrust may take, and of the different degrees to which some form of confrontational dissent may materialize as disloyalty or not, and be regarded, therefore, as defensible or not.

Dissent is not disloyalty. Whistle blowing raises squarely the problem of conflict of loyalties. Failure to provide *affectio societatis* is a mild but toxic form of disloyalty. As for the myth of a state clergy that is congenitally loyal, so that disloyalty can be declared impossible, it may be regarded as nothing but a clever subterfuge to avoid the question at hand. But this subterfuge is built on untenable foundations.

The virtue of dissent

My main argument may have left the impression that disloyalty is always a vice. Indeed, most of the time it is. But I feel a need, as a person who has made subversion his trademark, to take a moment to somewhat delimit the terrain of reprehensible disloyalty from the one of creative and justifiable dissent.

Dissent is not disloyalty. Jones and Sunstein have shown that there is strong pressure to conform in most situations. Yet conformism is not unlike free-riding: it benefits from the actions of others without adding anything (Sunstein 2003: 12). This is why real learning is unlikely to occur in an organization where everyone agrees with everyone else, and why well-functioning organizations and societies benefit from a wide range of views.

In the better old days, much of the work of a democracy was accomplished through robust dialectics of the elected official and of the expert bureaucrat. They both had legitimacy (representation and expertise) and it was felt that, through their dialogue and tense interaction, some workable governing would ensue. Canada lived through such a period in the mid-20th century (Hubbard and Paquet 2008). Dissent was often recorded between politicians and bureaucrats, but it was well understood that the views of the elected officials should prevail.

One of the most interesting developments of recent times (and one that explains the popularity of the word *governance*) is the significant erosion of the legitimacy of both politicians and bureaucrats. Bureaucrats no longer have the monopoly of moral and professional legitimacies of yesteryear. They are only one of the many expert voices. The same may be said about the electoral process: it no longer automatically grants legitimacy to elected officials (Rosanvallon 2008: 111ff). The governed have become directly involved in various ways, and have expressed their dissent in effective ways by constructing a true *contre-démocratie* (Rosanvallon 2006). The dissent of the governed has materialized in a more diffuse and less theatrical way than officialdom, but it has become quite effective in shaping governance (Carter 1998; Angus 2001).

Yet it is fascinating to observe that, despite the immense broadening of the range of legitimate stakeholders, many of the stylized debates in political science and public administration remain focused on the old dual system of the dialectics of politicians and bureaucrats, as if it were still the focal point of governing. In fact the whole governance *problématique* (claiming that there are many producers of governance) has been shunned, because it redefines the whole notion of the political to include many more actors and experts, interacting in many more loci.

Even within this reductive contested arena of bureaucrats and politicians, there has been a shift in the rules of the game. Instead of negotiated compromises, with the politicians having the final say, a substantial element of the bureaucracy has begun to claim that its expertise, professionalism, and disinterested character provides it with a stronger and more credible basis to provide a more legitimate definition of the public good than the one suggested by those churned out by the electoral process.

Disloyalty emerges when it becomes clear that some senior bureaucrats are unwilling to accept that the final say will go to the politicians, and when they are willing to actively pursue and relentlessly promote, through passive or active sabotage, their own version of what they presumed to be the public good. This entails not only dissent, but a redefinition of their burden of office, in such a way that the bureaucrats appear not to feel compelled to dedicate their full creative attention to the realization of what the politicians want to pursue. This may not mean active sabotage (although in some case it does), but often making simply a tepid *pro forma* contribution in the search for the best possible way to effect a policy or decision they do not agree with.

The dissent of the governed plays a crucial role in participatory democracy. It brings new actors onto the political scene, and "it makes questionable what has previously not been questioned and thereby opens up large areas of social life to public discussion, decision and action … [and] expands the options discussed within the public sphere where decisions are made and thus alters and renews the arena of democratic decision-making" (Angus 2001: 65-66). This sort of social criticism generates the creative energy required by a healthy democracy. It triggers social movements that are in turn "the crucible for the emergent publics" (*Ibid.*: 83).

Such dissent may be regarded as creative 'disloyalty' toward both establishment and institution. Graham Greene spoke in 1948 of "the virtue of disloyalty" (quoted by Holloway 2008) in defining the role of artists and other stakeholders, who do most to help institutions adapt to the change and flux of time because they are the least loyal to them.

Obviously this cannot be interpreted as a plea for disloyalty without limits, one that would lead to anarchy and a world of anything goes. Any meaningful definition of the burden of office entails a duty of loyalty, and the erosion of such a duty (as may occur unwittingly with the dilution of the rules in good currency) may be consequential. This is why the decline of the duty of loyalty in corporate law has been bemoaned (Brown 2006-07). Loyalty is the intrapersonal analogue of obedience (Falkenberg 1988), and it presumes that loyalty and obedience are agreed to from the start. So it may be more accurate to restate the Graham Greene phrase as "the virtue of dissent," to ensure that there is no ambiguity.

Whistle-blowing

In many quarters, whistle-blowing is celebrated disloyalty. In this case, there is not only dissent about what is acceptable and can be done, but action taken to denounce action that is purported to be violating well-understood and agreed upon principles even though such denouncing stands in violation of a duty of loyalty to one's superior.

Disloyalty to the superior is clearly warranted if the actions of the superior are in violation of the law, or explicit regulation, or endangering third parties. There is a trade-off between loyalties to the superior as opposed to loyalty to principles protecting the population or the organization from risks. No loyalty is absolute. The central question has to do with the nature of the trade-off. But one should be careful in defending the logic underlying whistle-blowing. If it were to serve as a reference, there would be no basis to argue for a duty of loyalty. It would be by definition contingent, since it can always be overridden by a superior duty. Since such a matter is a question of personal judgment, it is not clear that any disloyalty exists if one can be persuaded *en son âme et conscience* that what is done by a supervisor or minister is not in keeping with what he feels is best for the country.

Such logic would make it a matter of personal judgment (and by inference acceptable) for the subordinate to indulge in tactics that would delay the implementation of a policy or action that would not be, in his/her estimation, in the best interest of the country. This would amount to legitimizing all forms of disloyalty. Given the fact that whistle-blowing policies guarantee that whistle-blowers will not be punished, there would appear to be no limit to the damage that can be inflicted but by one's conscience. This could be immensely dangerous.

The only way to determine if such action is warranted is an *ex post* examination of the complaint, to determine if indeed the denounced action is in violation of law and regulation. But this makes current law and regulation, in its present form, into something absolute, and presumes that a proactive denunciatory defence of law and regulation, as they stand, is the accepted norm. Again, this may be unduly restrictive.

This *malaise* is all the more important since whistle-blowing need not be inspired by high-ground feelings, but may have its source in spite, or malice. It may also be based on false information, or an abusive interpretation of law and regulation, and can create much personal irreparable damage to the party under attack by a party that is promised impunity to begin with, if he/she comes forward with a denunciation.

It becomes clear that the *malaise* surrounding whistle-blowing (from all sides), and the fact that it is both celebrated as an act of courage and loyalty to the higher good, but also still considered as an act of disloyalty, makes such act only evaluable in context. It may or may not be disloyal, depending on circumstances.

The law has often determined that in certain circumstances (like crimes against children) those who are aware of what is going on and do not come forward may be charged. This is the logic behind the whole world of criminal negligence ("unsettling or rash lack of concern" as per the Criminal Code). Yet it is far from clear under what conditions one can speak of "unsettling and rash lack of concern."

It is for good reasons that one does not find a generalized celebration of 'ratting' or *délation* in good currency. There is still a certain stigma attached to *délation per se*: It is only upon being satisfied that the loyalty to higher things fully legitimizes the disloyalty to lower things that comfort is regained.

Affectio societatis

Any form of organization is built on the assumption that those who choose to become associates have a will to engage and to contribute actively to the common work. In French law, this sort of spirit of collaboration has a name – *affectio societatis*. It is a most important element in corporate law: more or less capturing the fact that partners enter into a partnership in good faith, with a will to associate and a commitment that is consequential (Cuisinier 2008). In French law, failure to demonstrate *affectio societatis* may lead to the dissolution of the partnership.

This presumption may give heartburn to quantophreniacs, but it has proved an important foundational aspect of French law, and has turned out to be more operational than would first appear.

As a constitutive element of organizations, *affectio societatis* entails that active and creative contribution to the association or partnership is expected, is part of a postulated moral contract, and is, therefore, part of the associates' burden of office. A delinquent associate (i.e., one failing to provide *affectio societatis*) is in breach of contract, and is failing to live up to his burden of office. Consequently, shirking is not only the source of X-inefficiency, but a way of failing the test of *affectio societatis,* and a form of disloyalty that can have grave consequences.

This particular phenomenon triggers very interesting considerations.

First, it underlines the fact that disloyalty may be the result not only of acts of commission, but also of acts of omission. This is similar to failure of doctors to provide help to persons in difficulty, or failure to provide professional defense to employees. These are regarded as reprehensible.

Second, it illustrates dramatically the fact that failure of engagement and commitment may be a form of disloyalty, whether or not it may result from shocks that have mitigated or attenuated the original commitment.

Finally, it forcefully makes the point that the burden of office, as a nexus of moral contracts, may be difficult to define, but that its very existence may suffice to determine if there has been disloyalty. Breaking a moral contract is disloyalty.

The myth of the state clergy

A most fascinating strategy to immunize state workers from being accused of disloyalty has been in good currency in public administration circles for quite a long time. It has taken the form of declaring state workers not, as Hugh Segal (2010) suggests, as being concerned first with public administration and its privileges, but (1) as mainly motivated by the public good; (2) as being charged with different, higher-order, and nobler tasks than other beings; and (3) as having been chosen for those tasks on the basis of exceptional qualities enabling them to respond to this calling.

Jane Jacobs (1992) has stylized this Manichean view of the world very aptly in her book *Systems of Survival*, in which she contrasts the public and the private spheres as corresponding to two very distinct sorts of activities, characterized by two syndromes: *the guardian moral syndrome* and *the commercial moral syndrome*. In her worldview, the public sector employees are guardians of the public good, and characterized in so doing as being ostentatious, adhering to tradition, showing fortitude, being obedient, disciplined and loyal, but also (since nothing is perfect) as dispensing largesse, making rich use of leisure, taking vengeance, and indulging in deception for the sake of the task. This is contrasted with the lower-order world of private sector employees as traders engaged in commercial activities and characterized in so doing as being honest, efficient, industrious and collaborative, respecting contracts, and being open to novelty and dissent for the sake of the task.

In the Jacobsian universe, those two worlds are not only contrasted, but should remain entirely separate. Public purpose and private gain are incompatible, and therefore should never mix, for what would ensue then would be 'monstrous hybrids.'

Jacobs' book was on the desks of most Ottawa senior bureaucrats in the early 1990s. It provided the intellectual argumentation in support of the special status being claimed by public servants as a group of persons dedicated to the public good, rather than being simply busy, like other workers, with private endeavours. This special status obviously called for special treatment, for the public sphere was purported to be not only different in degree from the private sphere, but as different in kind. Such a view is not only of historical interest; it is currently still propounded by senior academics in publications generated under contract financed by the Canadian public service (Kernaghan 2007).

This view of the world has had important impacts on Canadian political culture. It explains the visceral opposition to a private sector presence in health care, and to public-private partnerships, etc. It has also underpinned the view that not everyone is suitable for these higher-order tasks. Public sector employees are presented as chosen only because they have the exceptional qualities required to respond to this calling – for public service is a vocation, not a job. Indeed, we are informed that the Treasury Board Secretariat is preparing a joint venture with public administration academics to defend this special status of a state clergy.

For Jacobs, despite superficial similarities in the nature of the tasks carried out by employees of the public and private sectors, the differences are fundamental: public servants as an embodiment of the Hegelian State *sortent de la cuisse de Jupiter*. In that view of the world, the expression "disloyalty of public servants" is an oxymoron, a contradiction in terms. Public servants are the new state clergy, and loyalty is consubstantial to their very being – loyalty to the pursuit of the public good, a task for which they are obviously much better suited than the non-descript bunch of individuals delivered by the electoral process. Or so one might be led to conclude.

I was never very taken by Jane Jacobs' view of the world. It has always appeared to be extremely simplistic, naïvely Manichean, and perilously misleading: simplistic because it occludes civil society and reciprocity – this is not a two but multi-party game; Manichean, because it denies what governance studies have explored over the last few decades – the richness and effectiveness of inter-sectoral collaboration; misleading, because it provides an unwarranted sanctimonious blessing to public sector activities, *per se*. It is hardly surprising that this conceptualization has been seized upon by the bureaucracy as a gift of the Gods. But it miserably fails any test of reasonableness.

One of the many perverse unintended consequences of Jacobs' stylization is that it has provided moral support for an anti-democratic push by the public managerial class to usurp the dominium of the elected officials, and for a displacement of democratic values by professional/corporatist values in the ethical fabric of the Canadian federal public sector. Indeed, this has led to both democratic and professional values being conflated and confounded in the emerging version of the code of ethics of the Canadian federal public service, leading one to feel that the former are slowly *phagocytées* by the latter. It is hardly surprising that the political-bureaucratic interface has been tilted.

The impact of these developments on the disloyalty debate is important. By significantly strengthening the legitimacy of the bureaucracy (and professional values), and thereby significantly reducing the relative valence of the politicians (and thereby democratic values), the recent developments have contributed much to the attenuation and declawing of the notion of disloyalty. Bureaucratic judgment is openly allowed to challenge the legitimacy of the judgment of elected officials (Paquet 2014).

Conclusion

This chapter had two main ambitions: to provide a philosophical map of what is meant by disloyalty, and to put forward the hypothesis that there has been an increase in disloyalty in the Canadian federal public service.

On the first front, I hope to have enriched the notion of disloyalty somewhat, and to have extracted it from the 'closet of topics unsuitable for discussion.'

Whether my philosophical map will prove useful is, however, something that remains to be seen. My test of this has a Schumacherian flavour. As Fritz Schumacher explained (1977: 7), "mapmaking is an empirical art that employs a high degree of abstraction but nonetheless clings to reality." Type I, or so-called scientistic mapmakers, have a basic principle: in case of doubt, leave it out. Type II pragmatic mapmakers (i.e., mapmakers of my sort) take a different approach – like Schumacher, they suggest turning this principle into its opposite – and to work on the basis of the guiding principle: if in doubt, show it prominently.

The cost of this second approach is not that high since, if 'it' does not exist, someone will quickly show it to be not true. It happens within days on Wikipedia. On the other hand, the benefits may be high. The logic is simple: if one limits oneself to what is true beyond doubt, one minimizes the risk of error, but at the same time one maximizes the risk of missing out on what might be most important (*Ibid.*: 3).

On the second front, I am sure that there will be complaints that I have not provided the smoking gun, and that my 'demonstration' has failed to meet the standards of what Princeton University statistician John Tukey used to call colloquically the *interocular trauma test* – generating findings that hit the researcher, the reader and the audience between the eyes. That much I concede.

References

Akerlof, George A. 1984. *An Economic Theorist's Book of Tales.* Cambridge, UK: Cambridge University Press.

Angus, Ian. 2001. *Emergent Publics.* Winnipeg, MB: Arbeiter Ring Publishing.

Brown, J. Robert. 2006-07. "Disloyalty without Limits: 'Independent' Directors and the Elimination of the Duty of Loyalty," *Kentucky Law Journal*, 95(1): 53-105.

Carter, Stephen L. 1998. *The Dissent of the Governed.* Cambridge, MA: Harvard University Press.

Cuisinier, Vincent. 2008. *L'affectio societatis.* Paris, FR: Lexis-Nexis Litec.

Directors of Personnel. 1994. "The Way Ahead for the Public Service." Discussion paper for the Directors of Personnel Conference, Cornwall, ON, October 4-6.

Ewin, Robert E. 1993. "Corporate Loyalty: Its Objects and Its Grounds," *Journal of Business Ethics*, 12: 387-396.

Falkenberg, Gabriel. 1988. "Insincerity and Disloyalty," *Argumentation*, 2: 89-97.

Gigerenzer, Gerd. 2001. "The Adaptive Toolbox" in G. Gigerenzer and R. Selten (eds.). *Bounded Rationality: The Adaptive Toolbox.* Cambridge, MA: MIT Press, p. 37-50.

Gigerenzer, Gerd. 2007. *Gut Feelings – The Intelligence of the Unconscious.* New York, NY: Viking.

Giles, David E.A. and Lindsay, M. Tedds. 2002. *Taxes and the Canadian Underground Economy.* Toronto, ON: Canadian Tax Foundation Paper # 106.

Gladwell, Malcolm. 2005. *Blink: The Power of Thinking without Thinking.* New York, NY: Little, Brown and Co.

Gordon, H. Scott. 1961. *The Economists versus the Bank of Canada.* Toronto, ON: Ryerson Press.

Hardin, Russell (ed.). 2004. *Distrust.* New York, NY: Russell Sage Foundation.

Hirschman, Albert O. 1970. *Exit, Voice and Loyalty – Responses to Decline in Firms, Organizations and States.* Cambridge, MA: Harvard University Press.

Holloway, Richard. 2008. *Creative Disloyalty.* Essay presented to the Scottish Arts Council, May 9.

Hubbard, Ruth. 1995. "A Vision of the Future," *Ottawa Citizen*, May 14, A2.

Hubbard, Ruth and Gilles Paquet. 2007 "Cat's Cradling: APEX Forums on Wicked Problems," *www.optimumonline.ca*, 37(2): 12-18.

Hubbard, Ruth and Gilles Paquet. 2008. "Clerk as révélateur: a panoramic view" in P. Dutil (ed.). *Searching for Leadership: Secretaries to Cabinet in Canada*, Toronto, ON: Institute of Public Administration of Canada, p. 85-120.

Hubbard, Ruth and Gilles Paquet. 2009. "Design Challenges for the Strategic State: Bricolage and Sabotage" in A.M. Maslove (ed.). *How Ottawa Spends 2009-2010.* Montreal and Kingston: McGill-Queen's University Press, p. 89-114.

Hubbard, Ruth and Gilles Paquet. 2010. *The Black Hole of Public Administration*. Ottawa, ON: University of Ottawa Press.

Innerarity, Daniel. 2002. *La démocratie sans l'État*. Paris, FR: Climats.

Jacobs, Jane. 1992. *Systems of Survival*. New York, NY: Random House.

Jones, Stephen R.G. 1984. *The Economics of Conformism*. Oxford, UK: Blackwell.

Juillet, Luc and Gilles Paquet. 2002. "The Neurotic State" in G.B. Doern (ed.). *How Ottawa Spends 2002-03 – The Security Aftermath and National Priorities*. Don Mills, ON: Oxford University Press, p. 25-45.

Keen, Peter G.W. 1998 "Transforming Intellectual Property into Intellectual Capital: Competing in the Trust Economy" in N. Imperato (ed.). *Capital for our Times*. Stanford, CA: Hoover Institution Press, p. 3-35.

Kekes, John. 1993. *The Morality of Pluralism*. Princeton, NJ: Princeton University Press.

Keller, Simon. 2007. *The Limits of Loyalty*. Cambridge, UK: Cambridge University Press.

Kernaghan, Kenneth. 2007. *A Special Calling: Values, Ethics and Professional Public Service*. Ottawa, ON: Canada Public Service Agency.

Laurent, Paul and Gilles Paquet. 1998. *Epistémologie et économie de la relation – coordination et gouvernance distribuée*. Paris/Lyon, FR: Vrin.

Leibenstein, Harvey. 1976. *Beyond Economic Man*. Cambridge, MA: Harvard University Press.

Leibenstein, Harvey. 1987. *Inside the Firm*. Cambridge, MA: Harvard University Press.

Levine, John M. and Richard L. Moreland. 2002. "Group Reactions to Loyalty and Disloyalty," *Group Cohesion, Trust and Solidarity*, 19: 203-228.

Lindquist, Evert and Gilles Paquet. 2000 "Government Restructuring and the Federal Public Service: The Search for a New Cosmology," in E. Lindquist, (ed.). *Government Restructuring and Career Public Services in Canada.* Toronto, ON: Institute of Public Administration of Canada, p. 71-111.

Mesthene, Emmanuel G. 1970. *Technical Change.* New York, NY: Mentor Books.

Noer, David M. 1993. *Healing the Wounds.* San Francisco, CA: Jossey-Bass.

Paquet, Gilles. 1989 "The Underground Economy," *Policy Options,* 10(1): 3-6.

Paquet, Gilles. 2007. Background paper prepared for the Task Force on Governance and Cultural Change in the RCMP.

Paquet, Gilles. 2008. *Gouvernance: mode d'emploi.* Montreal, QC: Liber.

Paquet, Gilles. 2009a. *Scheming virtuously: The road to collaborative governance.* Ottawa, ON: Invenire Books.

Paquet, Gilles. 2009b. *Crippling Epistemologies and Governance Failures: A Plea for Experimentalism.* Ottawa, ON: University of Ottawa Press.

Paquet, Gilles. 2013a. "The Political-Bureaucratic Interface: A Comment on Andrew Griffith's Expedition," *www. optimumonline.ca,* 43(4): 61-74.

Paquet, Gilles. 2013b. "La gouvernance, science de l'imprécis," *Organisations & Territoires,* 21(3) : 5-17.

Paquet, Gilles. 2014. "Super-bureaucrats as *enfants du siècle," www.optimumonline.ca,* 44(2): at press.

Paquet, Gilles and Lise Pigeon. 2000. "In Search of a New Covenant," in E. Lindquist, (ed.). *Government Restructuring and the Future of Career Public Service in Canada,* Toronto, ON: Institute of Public Administration of Canada, p. 475-498.

Public Service Commission of Canada. 1994-95. *Annual Report.* http://resources.library.upei.ca/govdocs/SC1/SC1-1995.pdf [Accessed April 29, 2014].

Rosanvallon, Pierre. 2006. *La contre-démocratie*. Paris, FR: Seuil.

Rosanvallon, Pierre. 2008. *La légitimité démocratique*. Paris, FR: Seuil.

Rynor, Becky. 2009. "Rising workplace disloyalty 'no big surprise': expert." *Ottawa Citizen*, July 14.

Safire, William. 1994. "The New Disloyalty," *New York Times*, September 26.

Savoie, Donald J. 2003. *Breaking the Bargain*. Toronto, ON: University of Toronto Press.

Segal, Hugh D. 2010. "Beyond Centralization: How to Liberate Federalism?" in Ruth Hubbard and Gilles Paquet (eds.). *The Case for Decentralized Federalism*. Ottawa, ON: University of Ottawa Press, p. 93-115.

Schumacher, E.F. 1977. *A Guide for the Perplexed*. New York, NY: Harper & Row.

Sunstein, Cass R. 2003. *Why Societies Need Dissent*. Cambridge, MA: Harvard University Press.

Thomas, Paul G. 2009. Who Is *Getting the Message? Communications at the Centre of Government*. Research study for the Oliphant Commission.

Tussman, Joseph. 1989. *The Burden of Office*. Vancouver, BC: Talonbooks.

Part III
On The Canadian Scene

It would be both unhelpful and wrong to suggest that the social learning disabilities revealed in Parts I and II are condemning our socio-economies to be irretrievably poorly understood and governed. There are ways to overcome these liabilities, but it would be equally criminally irresponsible to disregard the bad habits of the mind, the intellectual laziness, and the unwillingness to explore outside of a certain zone of comfort that have prevented a vast majority of the social scientists from effectively tackling the problems facing Canada.

Mental prisons and flawed inquiring systems, and the like, have also prevented a clearer diagnosis and a more effective redesign of the organizational and institutional fabric from emerging. But this is not to say that such diagnoses and redesigns have been entirely absent.

In chapter 5, a synthetic diagnosis of the present Canadian *malaise* is proposed, based on work done at the Centre on Governance at the University of Ottawa.

Chapter 6 is a sketch of the lifework of one of Canada's social scientists who has followed a different path. It is presented as evidence that there are ways to probe the socio-economy synoptically with a view to redesigning it so as to make it more effective and resilient. Tom Courchene's work has been heterodox, and has led to bold and imaginative proposals for redesign. It may have had neither the impact nor the recognition it deserves, but it provides living proof that the tradition of transdiciplinary inquiring work, attempting to escape from the toxic mental prisons, and to build on integrative thinking and innovative social architecture, has survived.

The fact that this sort of work outside the mainstream has not challenged the citadels of disciplinary worldviews may be depressing, but the fact that it has survived must be taken as a sign that a renaissance of this sort of critical and design thinking is not impossible.

CHAPTER 5

| On The Canadian *Malaise*[1]

"Cela se prononce comme on a peur de l'écrire … "
Jacques Perret

Introduction

According to the Environics Institute FOCUS 2012 survey results, a majority of Canadians believes the country is heading in the right direction, expresses increased confidence in their system of government, and comparatively "less concern," "continued comfort" and "less worry" than citizens of other countries about most aspects of their lives.

But when Robin Higham and I began to probe below the surface of these celebratory results, we found a very large number of paradoxical and disquieting fault lines that echoed hardly the overall tale of the survey results, and that would appear to be systematically kept out of Canadians' consciousness: the largest yet recorded cleavage between Quebecers (34 percent) and other Canadians (83 percent) expressing a sense of pride in being Canadian; boasting confidence in the health care system, despite a large number of serious studies pointing to an imminent crisis situation – and consequently considerable reluctance in the citizenry to agree to any sort of fundamental reform; a similar schizophrenia and denial that any change is required in the face of the impending

---

[1] This chapter was co-authored with Robin Higham.

pension crisis; paradoxical support for the current high level of immigration concomitant with high and increasing concern that immigrants integrate less and less well economically, and do not adopt Canadian mores, etc. On all these fronts (and there are many more) there is a certain culture of contentment and, even when significant concerns break through the citizen's denial system and are reluctantly acknowledged, it would appear that they trigger no commitment to significant correctives. Contentment and inertia prevail.

Although the regional and local media are filled with news reports about the significantly defective functioning of the material and social fabrics of our socio-economy – from decrepit infrastructure, ineffective education and health care systems, serious problems of social integration, etc. – these warning signals are occluded nationally, and there appears to be no pressure from the citizenry, and no taste among the governing circles to even acknowledge the need for significant repairs.[2]

Few appear ready to acknowledge the possibility that a major disease has struck our democratic societies: blinding them to threatening realities, making them vulnerable to programming, and leaving them, because of an induced lethargy,[3] unwilling and unable to respond to the toxic circumstances that promise irreversible harm.

---

[2] Canada is not necessarily the only country in this situation. A recent document has highlighted the sort of frightening information available weekly in local and regional media in France that never gets reported in national media and, therefore, never seems to permeate the national consciousness. It showed an immense gap between reality and what one can only regard as the manufactured national percepts (Obertone 2013). While the situation might not be as dramatic in Canada yet, the same degree of cognitive dissonance and willful blindness may be said to exist here.

[3] This lethargy translates into cognitive dissonance and leads to the conclusion that no immediate action is required. The only groups that have vehemently denounced this willful blindness (and the brainwashing efforts to engineer and to rationalize it) are quickly demonized, especially when they expose such dysfunction as the result of some *malignant narcissism* (Bruce 2004) – or some *politics of guilt* (Gottfried 2002). Dysfunction is in any case generally denied.

Why is there so little that we are willing to do now in the face of predictable catastrophic outcomes? Worse still, what might we offer as an explanation when our grandchildren ask – and they will – why we have failed to be more responsible trustees of their future?

It is the view of some of us that the cumulative effect of the fading of critical thinking, of the weaknesses of the inquiring systems in good currency, and of the enfeebling of social learning and governance processes as a result of the toxic effect of mental prisons like quantophrenia, and of failures in collaboration, like disloyalty, has been catastrophic. It has entailed for Canada a large number of unmet challenges, and predictable irreversible damage in the making for our society.

In this short chapter, the objective is first to draw attention to a small sample of situations, bearing omens of predictable irreversible damage in the making, that both citizens and governments seem to willfully refuse to recognize; second, to look into the assemblage of psycho-social systemic slippages that might be responsible for this negligence that is likely to lead to impending tragedies; third, to hint at the foreseeable toxicity of this cascade of slippages if the syndrome of neglect prevails; and fourth, to suggest some initiatives to awaken the citizenry from its collective sleepwalking.

A sample of sources of concern

Whether the governance failures are ascribable to *malignant narcissim* or to some *politics of guilt*, or to a nexus of other forces, there is no doubt that Canada is failing to acknowledge crucial problems, and to respond effectively and creatively to a number of basic challenges. Our intent is not to produce an exhaustive catalogue of all such unmet challenges, but to underline a few critical situations commonly regarded as likely to become disastrous, and about which failure to respond is flagrant.

The first unmet challenge concerns our abysmal performance on the productivity and innovation front. Studies by the Centre for the Study of Living Standards and the Conference Board of Canada have shown that while productivity growth allowed the standard of living of Canadians to double every 18 years from 1947 to 1973, it is now growing four times more slowly and, as a result, the standard of living is likely to double only every 70 years. As for innovation, since the 1980s, Canada is rated D by the Conference Board, and ranks 14th out of the 17 industrialized countries examined by the board (Hubbard and Paquet 2011). Failing to recognize the dramatic impact that these congenital weaknesses in the Canadian socio-economy are bound to have on the future welfare of Canadians, and to take action to deal effectively with them is evidence of criminal negligence.

A second unmet challenge has to do with the refusal to face the impending crisis facing our health care and retirement pension systems. The cognitive dissonance of the citizenry, and the carelessness and lack of courage of governments in responding to it by implementing any of the repairs suggested by innumerable expert panels, make it hardly surprising that Canadians continue to praise the extraordinary superiority of their systems at the very moment that these systems are giving clear signs of imminent collapse (Hubbard, Paquet and Wilson 2012).

A third issue of concern is the failure to contain the flow of immigration into Canada within the bounds defined by the country's absorptive capacity – economic, financial, social – and to ensure that the waves of new arrivals do not erode the common public culture. In this case – as in many others – it may not be simple negligence, but rather deliberate willful deception by some politicians and the technocracy, with the complicity of the intelligentsia and the media. This deception has been ascribed by some observers to either presume collective guilt about the past, or to take on duty to atone for such a past. It has led to technocratic and media efforts 'to pathologize' critical attitudes and views by placing them outside of public discussion (Gottfried 2002: 95). These groups can legitimately be accused of the effective brainwashing of the citizenry about the putative benefits of mass immigration, and of irresponsibly propagandizing a multiculturalist ideology designed to blindside an intimidated populace, one that is afraid to be accused of nativism if they object to policies that are bound to dramatically undermine the fabric of Canadian society. Given the fragile nature of the common public culture in a liberal democracy like Canada, the damages perpetrated by such propaganda, since the 1990s, have been significant. These potential negative impacts have not only been denied, but those who have brought forth signals of distress have been defamed (Paquet 2012; Wente 2013).

A fourth unmet challenge concerns the erosion of Canadian citizenship, and the increasing *de facto* silent Balkanization of the country. The notion of citizenship has become so thin that it seems to have been reduced to a bouquet of entitlements. This has been engineered by the courts as a result of Charter cases, and has led to what Richard Gwyn (1995) called the "unbearable lightness of being Canadian." This, together with the Canadian multiculturalism policy, has brought about a degeneration of the country into a form of multitribalism, along with the judiciarization of intercultural interaction. The growing internecine strife among provinces and the loss of commitment to doing great things together – still a reference in the recent past (Underhill 1964) – are side effects of this erosion of citizenship that is weakening Canada's social fabric.

These problems are not uniquely Canadian in nature, but they are uniquely Canadian in the extent to which they are gleefully ignored. Indeed, the crux of our concern here is that Canadian governance appears to be blind to these sorts of problems, and incapable of considering that they call for urgent action – despite the fact that a significant portion of the most intellectually alert Canadians envisage that, if unchecked, many of these already detectable trends can lead only to catastrophes.

The central *malaise*, therefore, is not that these challenges exist and are acute, but that, in the case of Canada, there is an extraordinary capacity to deny their existence, and an extraordinary unwillingness to do anything about them.

Why such cognitive-dissonance-cum-inertia?

This is not a general explanation of the sort of inertia that one observes around the democratic world in modern times in the face of the slow erosion of some foundational pillars. It is too early to even tentatively suggest such grand schemes. Our intent here is more modest: to try to identify the sources of such blindness and inertia in Canada. We suggest that it is ascribable to a process of degradation of the common public culture as a result of the nexus of three families of forces: the installation of a culture of entitlement; the demise of critical thinking; and a certain cult of atonement.

Culture of entitlement[4]

In a world of surprises, accelerated change, and necessary adaptation to constantly changing circumstances, the quest for stability and certainty may be illusory, but it is nevertheless a constant human aspiration. Over time, the natural preference for not having one's life disturbed has come to be regarded as a widely-shared reasonable priority. This quest for stability has induced groups of citizens (with the complicity of governments, which are always seeking ways to please voters) to allow these preferences for certainty to be transubstantiated into some version of human rights, and those rights to be translated, in turn into the citizens' entitlement to have protection against undesirable circumstances provided by their governments.

With the Universal Declaration of Human Rights, the post-World-War II egalitarian doctrine argued that any citizen, *qua* citizen, is as meritorious and deserving as the next citizen, and this has made it possible for the view to emerge that any form of differential outcome is odious. Indeed, in radical circles, it has been argued that if one citizen cannot have access to a service, others should not have it either – in the name of equality of outcome. This means that entitlements have grown exponentially, and have come to be related not just to basic

---

[4] This section draws freely on an argument presented in chapter 4 of Gilles Paquet, *Tackling Wicked Policy Problems: Equality, Diversity and Sustainability* (2013).

needs, but also, and most vociferously, to *positional goods* (Hirsch 1976: 66): goods or services that are associated with a higher status. Envy has become a barometer of legitimate expectations, and any form of inequality denounced as fundamentally illegitimate. Such a view has been labeled 'progressive.'

Once preferences are re-labeled as rights and entitlements, they quickly crystallize into a set of guarantees that come to be regarded as having been earned (*des acquis*), and these preferences are expected to be satisfied by the state in perpetuity. Moreover, any existing platform of *acquis* in good currency at any one time quickly becomes the legitimate basis from which it can be expected that additional protections may be added in due time – down the wish list of the United Nations 1947 Universal Declaration of Human Rights, and more. This sort of progressive ratcheting up has acquired a certain sanctimonious merit, through systematic celebration as a fundamental and unchallengeable reference, so that any attempt to renegotiate previous arrangements in the light of changing circumstances, or of the discovery of unintended toxic consequences (financial or behavioural) of such arrangements, has come to be regarded as *de facto* unacceptable, whatever the reasons invoked.

The effect of some 50 years of such cumulative entitlements – what Nicholas Eberstadt (2012) has referred to as an "entitlement epidemic"– has been an exponential increase in state transfers to individuals, a growing dependency of citizens on such transfers, and the parallel growth of a culture of entitlement that would appear to make this growth likely to continue unabated. Toxic effects can be expected: on governments, for which this might become unaffordable; but also on the citizens themselves – for whom such arrangements may generate malefits in the form of learned dependency and helplessness, or an erosion of their burden of office as citizens, or even an erosion of their *moral character* and sense of responsibility as members of a liberal democracy.

Indeed, according to some observers, moral agency has already been undermined as governments have begun to take over tasks that individuals used to manage themselves. The very idea of *vulnerability* "has become such a cannibal that it now covers, not only the victims of misfortune or delinquency, but even the delinquents themselves" (Minogue 2010: 9).

The demise of critical thinking

This entitlement epidemic has contributed, at least in part, to the demise of critical thinking. As individuals developed a bloated notion of what they were entitled to, many of the arrangements that underpinned such an edifice became sacred cows. They were "placed outside public discussion" (Gottfried 2002), and immunized from any criticism as part of progressive arrangements: i.e., arrangements not necessarily rationally defensible on social, economic or political grounds, but regarded as legitimized by the hegemonic reference to compassion and, therefore, not to be questioned except perhaps by the odd *counter-progressive* – a condemnation without appeal as intellectually and morally deficient.

The notion 'progressive' has now permeated the conventional wisdom and immunized a whole range of policies and arrangements from any meaningful scrutiny. This has resulted in the exclusion of critical thinking from vast territories of public affairs.

When whole portions of human activity are out of bounds for critical thinking, ideologies run amok, and moral relativism becomes the new creed. Every judgment is made on the basis of ideology, and everything is as good as anything else, depending on the ideology invoked. No order of precedence is regarded as defensible, and any ordering at all is defined as contingent and illegitimate.[5] This new frame of mind has been vigorously propounded under all sorts of labels (post-modernism being the most celebrated), and any standard or ordering has come to be regarded as not more legitimate or worthy than any other.

There are problems generated by the failures to apply critical thinking to human affairs. Critical thinkers raise vital questions, formulate them clearly, gather relevant information and interpret it effectively, come to well-reasoned

---

[5] This decline in critical thinking has been documented in the public sector (Hubbard and Paquet 2014).

conclusions and decisions, test them on relevant criteria, think open-mindedly about alternative perspectives, assess their assumptions and consequences, and communicate effectively with others in coming to solutions.

As explained in chapter 1, critical thinking is "reasonable, reflective, responsible, and skillful thinking that is focused on deciding what to believe or do" (Schafersman 1991: 3). More analytically, critical thinking combines – *thinking skills* (analyzing, interpreting, explaining, evaluating, recognizing logical fallacies), *a skeptic's worldview* (recognizing that things are not always entirely what they seem), and *intellectual due process* (more integrity, humility, tolerance of uncertainty, and raw courage than most of us find easy to summon) (Gabennesch 2006).

As a result of generalized entitlements, and the deliquescence of all critical perspectives and reference points as contingent, the whole notion of critically appraising anything as better, or more valuable, than something else has been put into question. Given that opposition to anything is deemed simply the result of adopting a different ideology or perspective, presumed to be superior to the one in good currency, such opposition is summarily regarded as ill-founded and pretentious. It is hardly surprising, under such circumstances, if critical thinkers feel that they can enter the fray only at their peril.

Cult of atonement
The sense that any ordering is illegitimate and, therefore, the result of operations that are indefensible, has injected a sense of apprehended guilt into those tempted to call a spade a spade. Indeed, this sentiment has been distorted and exploited by the righteous few who make "a show of good conscience by apologizing for collective sins – and by exhorting the state to enact compulsory penance" (Gottfried 2002: 95). Self-censorship has emerged that has tended to emasculate public discourse, action and interaction. Indeed, apprehended denunciation, and the consciousness of having to expiate sins of critical thinking have begun to inhabit the public mind.

This has translated into behavioural modification of the most untoward sort: a sanitization of public language, a refusal to confront even the worst sophistry and deception, and a sheepish acceptance of even the most unreasonable accommodation in the name of tolerance – which is often a code word for the expiation for imagined sin.

Political correctness

This guilt at asserting any form of ordering or at suggesting any assessment of limitations and flaws in existing arrangements, or at pointing out the sources and causes of such flaws, has led to the language being purged of anything that might be regarded as sharp or stark statements about certain issues. Adverbs were mobilized to attenuate any statement to the point of making it trite and vacuous. Civility, which is the primary virtue enabling conversation and dialogue, was perverted to the point where it became a systematic avoidance of any critical view, and where all negative words were somewhat liquefied, so as to become meaningless. The first victim of this erosion of language was free speech and the banishment of contrarian views. The magic of dialogue was killed, and social learning was disempowered.

Failure to confront

Not only was language enfeebled, but action was neutered as well. Even the outrageous abuses of the rules of *vivre-ensemble* remain unchallenged. Challenges to the authority of the criminal code by Sharia promoters were narrowly defeated by Premier McGuinty's intervention; but on the other hand, there is the abject submission of Gatineau City Council – it withdrew a manual to help newcomers to better adjust to Canadian ways (prepared by the foreign-born and long-term Canadian resident city council member Mireille Apollon, in consultation with provincial officials). This action was taken on the sole basis of one immigrant's protest. How can we defend our ways of *vivre-ensemble* if no view can be regarded as more deserving than any other in our morally relativist world?

This, as might be expected, has led to ever more egregious abuses by groups who found that their very marginality would suffice to immunize them from sanction. Such hyper-tolerance has become incorporated in practices, and practices in rules. Over time, the fuss generated by any dissent has become sufficient to deter confrontation, however serious the matter in question.

Unreasonable accommodation

Perhaps even worse, because of the systematic failure to confront, there has been a silent refurbishment of the rules of *vivre-ensemble* in good currency to accommodate the most unreasonable requests. Traditions rooted in centuries of *vivre-ensemble* were blithely offered up as contingent nuisances, to be casually sacrificed in order not to offend one minority or another. This has led to a tyranny of the minorities: servile accommodation to the unreasonable wishes and preferences of marginal groups for the sole purpose of avoiding the confrontation that would bring with it automatic odium.

Some particularly vivid examples might be useful: the tolerance of polygamy in Bountiful, BC; the schools for 'Blacks-only' in Toronto; the refusal to monitor, during their period of qualification for citizenship, the true presence in Canada of persons with permanent resident requirements, etc.

A perfect quiet cultural capitulation[6]

The Canadian common public culture is a nebula. It is a compounding of the basic principles and essential beliefs that underpin the conventions and moral contracts that organize our *vivre-ensemble*. These principles and beliefs have developed over time, and represent the outcome of an evolutionary process blending both those factors inherited from our very humanity, as well as some more idiosyncratic features attached to our own organizational culture.

What made the Canadian case special is that Canadians, like many other societies, were not only swayed by the gospel of moral relativism, but they have come to be further swayed,

---

[6] This section borrows freely from some segments of chapter 3 in Gilles Paquet, *Moderato Cantabile: Toward Principled Governance for Canada's Immigration Policy* (2012).

so to speak, by propaganda: sufficiently to come to believe that not only is there no ranking of values, but also – and this is a quantum leap – no ranking of cultures either. One official would even state that Canada has no idiosyncratic ways of *vivre-ensemble*, no Canadian identity, "no national culture" of its own,[7] and that newcomers could therefore bring their own culture with them when migrating to Canada.

As a result, Canadians have unwittingly been led to sleepwalk into an erosion of their own evolving common public culture. Some of the intelligentsia, some political officials, and some of the media led the parade, and staunchly defended this equality of all cultures: that none could be superior to any other. This led naturally to the host society's indiscriminate accommodation of the cultures of illiberal newcomers. Even asking if there might not be limits to such accommodation – if, perhaps, elements of the host society's common public culture (e.g., gender equality) might legitimately be declared to be non-negotiable – has proved to be a controversial proposition. It is interesting to see how the mechanisms mentioned in the last section, working in tandem, have generated a dramatic storm that has left Canada in a precarious position.

The culture of entitlements has developed in Canada in a particular way – especially in the context of the 1982 Charter of Rights, which sidestepped any reference to responsibilities and duties; protected any newcomer entering Canada, legally or illegally; and was the subject of much judicial activism by the Supreme Court over the first decade of its life.

The full force of the multicultural ideology, for instance:

- as strengthened by Article 27 of the Charter, committing Canada to preserve and enhance the multicultural heritage of Canadians), and

---

[7] This astounding statement was made by Sheila Finestone in 1995 (then Secretary of State for Multiculturalism in the federal Liberal government of Canada) (quoted in Richard Gwyn, 1995).

- the political insouciance that greeted the Singh decision by the Supreme Court – the Canadian government did not dare to use the notwithstanding clause when the Supreme Court of Canada (by a three-to-three decision, i.e., one in which the Chief Justice had to cast the deciding vote) ruled in 1985 that a foreigner putting one foot on Canadian soil (legally or not) thereby acquired all the rights and privileges of Canadian citizens, except the right to vote (as per article 7 of the Charter), can only be ascribed to the Canadian *ethos* having evolved dramatically in real time under the noxious influences of the culture and politics of guilt.

The post-Charter decade gave rise to a frenzy of rights. During that period a Charter, which had been put in place to protect the citizen from undue state intervention, was transformed by identity groups into an instrument to create entitlements of all sorts. During the same period, the Supreme Court was not satisfied to interpret the law. It used the Charter to rewrite the law.

Through a series of decisions, reviewed by Gwyn:

- the Supreme Court ensured that article 15(2) of the Charter (about group rights) came to take precedence over article 15(1) that guaranteed individual rights;
- it dramatically extended the ambit of what might legitimately be regarded as a basis for Charter appeal by "disadvantaged groups," through an extraordinary broadening of the definition of "disadvantaged group," and a significant extension of the grounds for complaint to include anything that might connote "chilly climate" or "hostile environment" – whatever these words might mean; and,
- moreover, the courts in general came to accept as legitimate in their proceedings the notion of "cultural defence," based on self-proclaimed beliefs. In a world where most of the population might be able to claim being part of a "disadvantaged group," as it became so loosely defined, cultural defence based on self-

proclaimed cultural beliefs takes the law into a quagmire (Gwyn 1995: Part III, passim: 197).[8]

It is easy to see how, in the new post-Charter era, a culture of entitlements could flourish, identity politics could thrive, and diversity could come to be politicized. In this context, it became politically incorrect to criticize the new massive and indiscriminate immigration policy of both Liberal and Conservative governments. Indeed, such a regime was promoted as legitimate, acceptable, and even honourable and advantageous – a model for the rest of the world.

That new *ethos* helps to explain the reversal of Canadian views about immigration (as captured in the polls): from the mid-1970s to the mid-1990s, two thirds of the population felt generally that there might be too much immigration. But some 60 percent disagreed with this proposition in the following decade. Such a phenomenal reversal of perspectives (despite the fact that this was a period in which problems with integration were increasing and becoming common knowledge) deserves more attention than it has received. It most certainly revealed a high degree of false consciousness, a significant gap between the underlying socio-economic realities and the representations concatenated by the diversity/multiculturalism ideology that had been permeating public consciousness over the preceding decade or so. Indeed, the new ideology had become the new *Canada brand*, able to filtre out any inconvenient truth.[9]

[8] On January 13, 1994, a Canadian county court judge (Raymonde Verreault) could in all seriousness impose a reduced sentence on a man who had sexually assaulted his 11-year old stepdaughter over a two-year period, because he had only sodomized her, thereby (in the words of the judge) "preserving her virginity, which seems to be a very important value in their [Islamic] religion" (Gwyn 1995: 197).

[9] According to Paul Edward Gottfried (2002: passim, 8-14), much of it has been the result of the work of the therapeutic state reconstructing the consciousness. This would explain the puzzling shift of opinion over a relatively short time that was discussed extensively in Gilles Paquet, *Moderato Cantabile: Toward Principled Governance for Canada's Immigration Policy* (2012). All the mechanisms mentioned in the last section might have worked more explosively in the context of the post-Charter ebullition in Canada.

It was not until the second half of the first decade of the 21st century that expressions of concern began to be heard again, as the newcomers' increasing difficulties with integration, and the problems of reasonable and unreasonable accommodation demanded by some of the groups of newcomers revealed a growing apprehension about the impact of the large inflow of immigrants, not only on the socio-economy, but also on the common public culture. However, even over the last few years, these concerns have been expressed only *sotto voce* and anonymously in polls, because they remain unwelcome views in public fora. Serious studies about the costs of indiscriminate massive immigration are still savaged as nativist and xenophobic propaganda, and concerns about the impact of excessively large cohorts of newcomers on the common public culture are routinely squelched.

Through all those years, until recently, critical evaluations of the new immigration policy were met with scorn by the governments of the day, the technocracy, the intelligentsia and the media, while the messages of the 'choir' of immigration lawyers and multiculturalism lobbyists about such critical evaluations being racist and nativist were widely publicized. Indeed, this was usually supplemented in the media by an 'alternative explanation' for the new immigrants' increasing difficulties in smoothly integrating into the Canadian socio-economy. It was supposedly entirely due to Canada being a "systemically racist" society – according to a proclamation by Stephen Lewis in his 1992 Report on Racism to the Premier of Ontario. Atonement and self-flagellation had reached new heights.

This is only one area where the cascade of mechanisms was played out; they have also worked themselves into our collective life in many others. At the core of the threat to the common public culture is our willful blindness to its erosion, and to the long-term impact of defective arrangements, as well as the inertia of the governance apparatus: an unwillingness and incapacity to react and to repair these defects in the face of such challenges.

What to do?

It should be clear that some of these threats have come from the outside (as we have hinted at above), but most of them have come from the inside: from a culture of contentment and a sense of guilt.

This syndrome, which has not yet been blessed with a name, is responsible for both our willful blindness and our inertia in the face of irreversible slippages. Caught within the web of these various forces, no simple fix or gimmick will elicit a way out. What is required is a revolution of the mind, a different perspective, and refurbished governance.

What appears to be missing is, perspective-wise, a 'crane'; something which would send down a hook to lift the observer into a position where the perspective is *broadened* to take into account interactions, mind frames and power interfaces, *lengthened* to extend the time horizon, and *elevated* to transcend the contingent aspects of the citizens' daily lives. What is also missing is a governance apparatus that provides the motivation to deal with the challenges revealed by the view from the crane.

On the first front, it might be worth again considering a suggestion that has been floating about for almost 50 years: the creation of a *Committee on the Long Run* in the Senate of Canada,[10] which would ensure a fair dialogue about matters where predictable trends point to irreversibilities. It would generate the sort of mobilization of informed stakeholders that is necessary for such issues to be fully aired, described, and discussed, and for inquiries into effective wayfinding to be put into effect promptly.

In many issue domains, Senate committees have played that key role in Canada in the past. In earlier times, the reflective work of the Senate committees has often been translated into action rather quickly when the case could be made that the matter was urgent. The recommendations of

---

[10] The idea was mentioned explicitly in David Braybrooke and Gilles Paquet (1987). It was based on earlier suggestions made in the 1960s, first by Alvin H. Hansen (1960), later in the *Final Report of the Special Committee of the Senate Committee on Aging* (February 1966) and by Gilles Paquet (1968).

the Senate Committee on Aging of 1964 were in the Speech from the Throne in 1966. One cannot expect such a rapid connection between findings, recommendations, and action these days, since problems are often immensely more complex and unlikely to be tackled with one instrument. Yet even the ill-fated experiences of the visionary Senate Committee on Science Policy, piloted by Senator Maurice Lamontagne in the 1970s, or of the excellent work on health care by Senator Michael Kirby, have shown that these reports have prepared the ground in invaluable ways for the responses to come. In the case of such wicked problems, the transmission process from excellent research and recommendations to action can be daunting, if not completely intractable. An effective response cannot rest only on the sole power of good intellectual work and carefully crafted recommendations. What is needed, in addition, is an effective inquiring system designed to elicit experimentally the requisite social learning that will bring forth effective coordination, when power, resources and information are widely distributed among many hands and heads.

On this second front – the means to inquire fruitfully, and the motivation to deal with the challenges revealed by the view from the crane – we can no longer depend on the work of a single champion, as, for instance, when Senator Croll campaigned across the country, during the 1964-66 period, trying to persuade Canadians that the 1964 report of the Senate Committee on Aging had to be acted on swiftly. There will have to be some concerted action to carry the conclusions of the *Committee on the Long Run* to the range of social actors in the governance process most likely to ensure that appropriate action is indeed implemented.

This cannot be done without the help of a roundtable of relevant stakeholders being created to ensure that the process of mobilization and implementation is deployed with the huge arsenal of modern communications technology and social networks, so that the creative ideas put forward by the *Committee on The Long Run* are given a full national airing, and are allowed to be neither ignored, nor discarded lightly and irresponsibly. This would mobilize the creative work and imagination of the Senate as *animateur*.

There have been many complex thorny issues that have been handed to special committees or commissions in the past, with the result that Canadian life has been changed: some Senate committees, some royal commissions, some expert panels of the Royal Society of Canada, some investigative committees at the provincial level, etc. Some of those experiments have fizzled out or failed because of their amateurism or other flaws, but many have provided extraordinary experiments in problem redefinition and have changed the Canadian scene, even when they refused to issue a programmatic final report – e.g., the Royal Commission on Bilingualism and Biculturalism, which preferred to allow better informed Canadians, as a result of the Royal Commission's work, to distil their own responses at their own pace within the corridor of possible futures that had been mapped.

This is a task that would fit the Senate of Canada perfectly. It would provide it with a value-adding mission in the Canadian institutional fabric, and it would force the process of selecting senators to take some distance from the whimsicality that has generated the quilt-like nature of the current institution. There is an 'elite' of senators that can play this role now, and this portion could be improved upon, once it is known that those appointed will be asked to tackle the most difficult problems facing this country. We could then anticipate that no one called on to serve would be tempted to decline.

A double set of benchmarks would guide the processes of both exploration and implementation, sketched above. They are a balancing of:

- the imperatives of the cardinal virtues that carry with them the wisdom of the ages (*temperantia* – an awareness of the sense of limits; *fortitudo* – taking into account context and long term; *justitia* – a sense of what is good; and *prudentia* – what is practical and reasonable), and

- the basic principles (representative democracy, rule of law, etc.) and essential beliefs (freedom of choice, equality of men and women, equality of opportunity, etc.) defining the common public culture.

One would expect that the implementation phase would build on an inquiring system. It would seek to find ways to define the corridor of governance arrangements likely to ensure the development of the mix of incentives and moral contracts that are capable of generating both some detoxification of flawed arrangements, and some design of alternative social learning processes, promising more value adding (in the broadest sense of the term), innovation and progress.

Despite its fundamental optimism, such an approach is not utopian, and the misadventures of a few rogue senators should not be allowed to irretrievably doom an institution that has served Canadians very well in the past on this front.

Conclusion

What could kickstart such a process?

Charles Kindleberger, an eminent economic historian, has suggested that such transformations in socio-economies are so difficult that they are usually observed only in extraordinary circumstances, like wars or defeats that destroy the institutional fabric and force socio-economies to rebuild anew. The implications of such a view are clear: the challenge is nothing less than discovering or engineering the moral equivalent of a war, or the sociological equivalent of a defeat, in order to get an arterio-sclerotic socio-economy to rejuvenate itself (Kindleberger 1978). These are very daunting prerequisites.

No less taxing perhaps is the suggestion of Anthony Appiah, who has argued that most moral revolutions, like the abolition of slavery or the end of dueling – two examples of most destructive governance arrangements – have been triggered by a change in the code of honour (Appiah 2010), in the way the appreciation system was shaped, and the way in which the notion of what is honourable was defined.

It is possible that one of the side-effects of the work of a *Committee on the Long Run* will be to make Canadians aware of their responsibility for their grandchildren, and to shame them into a greater awareness of how dishonourable it is to neglect their fate. Much of the concern about environmental issues has already come to life in that manner. If citizens can be shamed into not asking for plastic bags at their grocery store, for the environment's sake, they might be mobilized into pressing for action to counter certain potential irreversibilities for the very essence of their country – if they are presented and understood as imperiling one's grandchildren. Inaction then would become a dishonourable choice.

A bit of irony might also be useful. Canadian citizens might be ironically reminded that if we were searching for a rallying call or a mock national anthem for Canadians – given the present level of contentment and inertia – *"tout va très bien, madame la marquise"* might be a suitable fit. It is the title of a 1935 song by Paul Misraki that marvelously captures a certain willful blindness in the face of catastrophe. It is the phone conversation between an aristocratic lady (who is out of town) with her valet who is at home in her castle. The valet keeps telling her everything is alright, except for a sequence of bad news that he communicates to her *seriatim* (from the death of her horse to the suicide of her husband). Each time, in between each new and more disastrous announcement, the chorus reiterates in a more and more absurd way ... *mais à part ça, madame la marquise, tout va très bien, tout va très bien.*

But the real starting point is the belief that we can develop such initiatives, that we can bring back into public discussion those attitudes, views and arrangements that used to be regarded as taboo topics. Therefore, we take consolation from independent thought crawling out of the blasted landscape (to quote a headline of the *National Post* of June 4, 2013), and topics like supply management, road tolls, the Rand formula, Native property ownership, carbon tax, even abortion ... begin forcing themselves into the public square and emerging from the most varied Canadian political corners (Coyne 2013). Or when we read on June 5th about John Baird's "dignity agenda" – defined by a former diplomat as an idealistic notion that just might be worth pursuing on the international scene (Robertson 2013). All this in the short space of two days! Readers might then understand why yesterday I might have been ready to conclude this paper by saying that I was not too hopeful, but that now I have hope, providing that we can unlock some of the mental prisons that have been unearthed.

Yet as if reality had decided to maul us, a headline on the front page of *The Globe and Mail* recently brought back, with a vengeance, a reminder of our unique Canadian toxic capacity to allow *malignant narcissism* to cripple our ways. It arrived in the form of the unilateral announcement by the French service of the Canadian Broadcasting Corporation (CBC) – Radio-Canada – a public broadcaster in the French language, richly funded by the Canadian federal government, that it would erase any reference to Canada in its new public face (Leblanc 2013). Such a decision should contribute, in our own remarkable and toxic Canadian way, to increasing yet again the "unbearable lightness of being Canadian," and constitute an explicit betrayal of the federal organization's mission in forging Canadian unity in diversity through better pan-Canadian communication.

Fortunately, the response to this petty ignominy, or act of sabotage, was not abject silence, as one might have feared, but the drawing of a line in the sand by Canadians and *Canadiens* who value their nationality, and who pay for this Canadian service – reminding the disloyal satraps responsible for this discourteous act of provocation that Canadian patience has limits, and that they have now been transgressed.

One can draw some optimism even from such small healthy reactions and victories.

References

Appiah, K. Anthony. 2010. *The Honor Code – How Moral Revolutions Happen*. New York, NY: Norton.

Braybrooke, David and Gilles Paquet. 1987. "Human Dimensions of Global Change: The Challenge to the Humanities and the Social Sciences," *Transactions of the Royal Society of Canada*, Fifth Series, Vol. II, p. 271-291.

Bruce, Tammy. 2004. *The Death of Right and Wrong*. New York, NY: Three Rivers Press.

Canada. 1982. "Charter of Rights and Freedoms," *Constitution Act, 1982*. http://publications.gc.ca/collections/Collection/CH37-4-3-2002E.pdf [Accessed May 1, 2014].

Coyne, Andrew. 2013. "Independent thought crawls out of the blasted landscape of Canadian politics," *National Post*, June 4.

Eberstadt, Nicholas. 2012. *A Nation of Takers – America's Entitlement Epidemic*. West Conshohocken, PA: Templeton Press.

Environics Institute. 2012. *Focus Canada 2012*. environicsinstitute.org/uploads/institute-projects/environics institute - focus canada 2012 final report.pdf [Accessed May 9, 2014].

Gabennesch, H. 2006. "Critical Thinking. What is it good for? (In fact, what is it?)," *Skeptical Inquirer*, 30(2): 36-41.

Gottfried, Paul Edward. 2002. *Multiculturalism and the Politics of Guilt*. Columbia, MO: University of Missouri Press.

Gwyn, Richard. 1995. *Nationalism without Walls – The Unbearable Lightness of Being Canadian*. Toronto, ON: McClelland & Stewart.

Hansen, Alvin H. 1960. *Economic Issues of the 1960s*. New York, NY: McGraw-Hill.

Hirsch, Fred. 1976. *Social Limits to Growth*. Cambridge, MA: Harvard University Press.

Hubbard, Ruth and Gilles Paquet. 2011. "Innovation and Productivity Policies as Inquiring Systems," *www.optimumonline.ca*, 41(4): 1-8.

Hubbard, Ruth and Gilles Paquet. 2014. *Probing the Bureaucratic Mind: About Canadian Federal Executives*. Ottawa, ON: Invenire Books.

Hubbard, Ruth, Gilles Paquet and Christopher Wilson. 2012. *Stewardship*. Ottawa, ON: Invenire Books, ch. 4-5.

Kindleberger, Charles P. 1978. *The Aging Economy*. Kiel: Institut für Weltwirtschaft.

Leblanc, Daniel. 2013. "CBC's French service name change to 'Ici' raises eyebrows in Ottawa," *The Globe and Mail*, June 6.

Lewis, Stephen. 1992. Report of the Advisor on Race Relations to the Premier of Ontario, Bob Rae. www.siu.on.ca/pdfs/report_of_the_advisor_on_race_relations_to_the_premier_of_ontario_bob_rae.pdf [Accessed May 1, 2014].

Minogue, Kenneth. 2010. *The Servile Mind*. London: Encounter Books.

Obertone, Laurent. 2013. *La France – orange mécanique*. Paris: Editions Ring.

Paquet, Gilles. 1968. "The Economic Council as Phoenix" in Trevor Lloyd and Jack McLeod (eds.). *Agenda 1970 –Proposals for a Creative Politics*. Toronto, ON: University of Toronto Press, p. 135-158.

Paquet, Gilles. 2012. *Moderato Cantabile: Toward Principled Governance for Canada's Immigration Policy*. Ottawa, ON: Invenire Books.

Paquet, Gilles. 2013. *Tackling Wicked Policy Problems: Equality, Diversity and Sustainability*. Ottawa, ON: Invenire Books.

Robertson, Colin. 2013. "John Baird's "dignity agenda" – an idealistic notion that just might work," *Communiqué of the Canadian Defence & Foreign Affairs Institute*, June 5.

Schafersman, S.D. 1991. *An Introduction to Critical Thinking*. http://facultycenter.ischool.syr.edu/wp-content/uploads/2012/02/CriticalThinking.pdf [Accessed May 24, 2014].

Senate of Canada. 1966. "Final Report of the Special Committee of the Senate Committee on Aging," *Debates of the Senate of Canada*, February 6, p. 79-80.

Underhill, Frank H. 1964. *The Image of Confederation*. Toronto, ON: Canadian Broadcasting Corporation.

Wente, Margaret. 2013. "Sweden's Immigration Consensus is in Peril," *The Globe and Mail*, June 1.

| On Tom Courchene as *Savanturier*

" ... il faudrait réhabiliter le métier d'entremetteur ..."
François Bott

Introduction

first provide a tiny bit of historical context for those who might either be too young to have been informed, or older but prematurely an amnesiac about the partial lobotomy suffered by the Canadian economic discourse in the latter part of the last century. Second, I review a small sample of Tom Courchene's extensive written work, illustrating his craft rather well. In conclusion, I add a succinct rumination on the disappearance of a tradition Courchene represents so well, and on what he might be able to do to keep it alive a bit longer.

Canadian economics and a prudent heretic

There was once a time when *Canadian economics* (quite different from 'economics in Canada') represented a discourse of import in this country. As the whole body of work of Harold Innis,[1] the task of working out a theory adapted to the situation in Canada was once regarded as a priority in Canada. Those were the days

---

[1] Harold Adams Innis (November 5, 1894-November 8, 1952) was a Canadian professor of political economy at the University of Toronto and the author of seminal works on media, communication theory and Canadian economic history, http://en.wikipedia.org/wiki/Harold_Innis.

when most social scientists were Deweyian – for them, as for John Dewey, in the beginning was the issue. I had occasion to reminisce about this era at the time of the 1992 celebration of the 25th anniversary of the creation of the *Canadian Economics Association* (Neill and Paquet 1993).

On that occasion, Robin Neill and I sketched the emergence of this Canadian economic discourse from the 19th century on, and its crystallization between 1920 and 1950. This was a discourse one might best characterize as an *économie engagée* that focused much on Canadian problems and institutions with a clear applied bent, and a whiff of skepticism about theory for the sake of theory.

But from the 1950s on, there was a significant paradigm shift: a shift from an interest in *content* to more and more of an interest in *method*, and a redefinition of economics as discipline. This was best captured in a 1967 paper by Harry Johnson (published in the first issue of the *Canadian Journal of Economics* in 1968) in which he proposed a much narrower notion of economics.

In his survey of meaningful contributions to economics in Canada, Johnson recognizes as such only "a piece of work of *general interest to the international profession* of economics" (1968: 129-146) (my emphasis). This was to become the beacon guiding the profession in Canada over the following decades.

From that time on, in Canada (but elsewhere as well), the profession has busied itself producing a stream of *"modls"* (a word invented by Axel Leijonhufvud to refer to implements produced by the profession, most of which would seem to be of little or no practical use – AL *dixit* – but quite important in determining the status of the individual in the profession). These implements have attracted appreciation and celebration in academic circles, but also some sarcasm (Leijonhufvud 1973).

Over the last few decades, there has been a modest rearguard surge of works refocusing on the socio-economy as an instituted process in Canada, mainly as a result of the work of heretics who have bucked the trend. Many of them are still in departments of economics, but most of them have taken refuge in specialized research institutes and units, schools of business or public policy, government agencies, consulting firms, etc. – where it may be said that much of the knowledge of the workings of the Canadian socio-economy is now developed.

Tom Courchene has been one of those heretics: a political economist, a diagnostician, a social architect, a public intellectual, but mostly a *savanturier* – a sort of clever crasis of the two words *savant* + *aventurier* invented by Raymond Queneau – a label that captures Courchene's nature most aptly. After a glorious life among the Econ,[2] he migrated to locales where political economy (akin to the old Canadian economics discourse) is still not only legitimate, but celebrated. It is improbable that Courchene would have had the impact he has had on the Canadian scene without this migration, and the support he received from extra-academic institutions.

Yet, and this is one of the particularities of Tom Courchene's professional career, he has remained *a very prudent heretic*, who has succeeded, through impressive navigational skill, in not ever being fully disowned by the canonical profession, while operating very clearly outside its mainstream. He owes this as much to his congeniality as to his deliberate non-abrasive style, but also to the fact that even colleagues for whom 'policy sucks' recognized his competence and scholarship, although they would not wish to join him in his adventurous voyages.

Une connaissance charnelle of the Canadian socio-economy

My mentor, Albert Faucher, used to say that to be a good social scientist one had to have *une connaissance charnelle* – a very intimate knowledge – of the socio-economy in which one lives. Otherwise, he would add, one would never be able to make sense of what is going on, or to understand the complex interactions

---

[2] His many books on Canadian monetary policy in historical perspective have become Canadian classics.

that underpin events and come up with meaningful diagnoses and practical repairs.

Courchene has been particularly good at this sort of ethnographic work. He has immersed himself in different environments, and invested much time and energy in developing his diagnostic skills by giving much attention to the art of description and contextual appreciation.[3] Many others have tried to look carefully, and yet have not seen what was there. Courchene has had a knack for identifying and extracting meaningful patterns, where others saw only a bunch of dots.

Let me review three samples of Courchene's written work.

First, his interesting forays into the challenges facing Quebec and Ontario in the late 1980s provide much evidence of Courchene as *diagnostician*.

Other most enlightening vignettes of interest are those proposed by Courchene about how one might design the *community of the Canadas*, and how one might find a way to insert the governance of the First Nations within the context of the Canadian political infrastructure as it stands. These vignettes illustrate Courchene's work as *social architect* – his trademark in many papers and books in the 1990s and early 2000s. These publications not only display some of his imaginative design work, but throw some light on Courchene's mode of reasoning.

Finally, Courchene, of late, has tried his hand at broader vistas. In some recent reflective and speculative papers, he has explored *futuribles* – possible futures. These papers have revealed Courchene as an *organizer* in the sense that Socrates was an organizer – one whose job is "to raise questions that agitate, that break through the accepted pattern" (Alinsky 1972: 72).

Quebec and Ontario

The pair of studies I am particularly interested in here were written in 1986-88: the first one in French, and the second one in English (Courchene 1987, 1989). These papers are exploring the psyche of Quebec and Ontario, respectively. These are unique

---

[3] The perils of crippling epistemologies grafted on poor descriptions have rarely been acknowledged but are quite important (Sen 1999: 139-145).

pieces – for I know of nothing else that quite succeeded in surveying this sort of territory at the time.

The piece on Quebec was written in the fall of 1986, when Courchene was Visiting Professor at *L'Ecole nationale d'administration publique* in Montreal. It seized the occasion of the publication of three Quebec government documents prepared by ministers in the Bourassa government – on privatization (Pierre Fortier), on the reform of government organizations (Paul Gobeil), and on deregulation (Reed Scowen) – and of the disquiet that these publications had generated at the time, to reflect on the dilemmas they appeared to reveal in the relationship between the citizen and the state in Quebec.

Courchene does more than simply summarize and evaluate these three reports. He uses them to gauge what he calls Quebec's drift toward a market nationalism stance. In those reports, Quebec would appear to be envisaging a move toward a more subtle, collaborative strategic state, in lieu of the more intrusive propulsive state that had been in good currency in Quebec since the early 1960s.

As these reports were not well received, Courchene speculated as to whether this unease is ascribable to their terse and technocratic tone (that failed to put their recommendations in context), or whether what these reports suggest may simply have been a wee bit too audacious and revolutionary to be palatable at the time. These documents underline a rebalancing of three fundamental social choices: between efficiency and security, decentralization and centralization, and the private and the public sectors – a move on all three fronts from an emphasis on the latter to an emphasis on the former. Courchene conjectured that Quebec might become a sort of unlikely *avant-garde* on these fronts, and that many other segments of the country might soon be following that lead.

Premier Bourassa developed an acute case of 'cold feet' in the face of the opposition the reports faced, so their thrust fizzled (Paquet 2008: 57-69). However, Courchene was bang on in identifying the dilemmas that Quebec was grappling with, and would continue to grapple with over the following decades.

Very soon afterward, Courchene used a cognate approach to frame his approach to the concurrent Ontario experience. He marshaled very surprising opinion poll results about the attitudes of persons in Quebec and Ontario at the time. For instance, to the question "Should there be substantially less government intervention in the economy?" a surprising 73 percent of Quebecers indicated that they would so prefer, while only 53 percent of Ontarians concurred; as to the question "Should Canadian governments de-emphasize social programs in favour of policies which encourage economic growth and investment?", 68 percent of Quebecers stated that they would so prefer, while only 43 percent of Ontarians concurred.

The psychoanalysis of Ontario that Courchene then undertook was aimed at understanding why Ontarians would appear to hold these views: he asked "what does Ontario want?" Daringly, after some reminders of the historical context, Courchene contrasted the *Peterson social agenda*[4] to the *Bourassa economic agenda* in the second half of the 1980s. He ascribed the contrast in part to Ontario's advantageous fiscal position, to some existential soul-searching in Ontario and much negative reaction to *Reaganism*,[5] and to some disquiet about the impending free-trade agreement with the United States.

In both those studies, Courchene is an *ethnographer plus*. He uses his economic outlook as an illuminating lamp, but casts a much wider political, sociological, cultural and psychological perspective on these terrains. This is Courchene the diagnostician at work.

Community of the 'Canadas,' First Nations' province, and a state of mind

In the 1990s, Courchene was no longer only an ethnographer and diagnostician: he transformed audaciously into a social architect, and the canvas on which he worked was ever expanding.

[4] The Hon. David R. Peterson served as premier of Ontario from 1985 to 1990.
[5] Refers to the attitude surrounding the economic policies of Ronald Reagan, 40th president of the United States, 1981-89.

Two short monographs published by the *Institute of Intergovernmental Relations* at Queen's illustrate Courchene's work as designer rather nicely.[6] They are both efforts to reframe and to re-engineer some aspects of Canadian federalism – a matter that would engage Courchene intensely over that period. The first scheme was presented at the Bélanger-Campeau Commission, and was a plan to re-constitute the 'Canadas' into a European-style community; the second proposes to boldly use a provincial approach to integrate First Nations' self-government into the traditional Canadian framework.

In both cases, Courchene presented the vision of new organizational forms that did not exist then but might be created. He sketched the broad outlines of these new entities.

This is not the usual testing of hypothesis mode, but a different mode of reasoning – neither deduction nor induction, but what some would call *transduction* – and others, *abductive* reasoning – exploring and groping for systems that did not yet exist and needed, in his opinion, to be designed (Romme 2003). This is a form of reasoning which starts from a sense that there is a gap to be filled, sketches a provisional prototype, and builds on a process of ongoing feedback that allows for refinement as the exploration proceeds – *design as the outcome of an inquiring system.*

This sort of intellectual operation may not have been in good currency in positivist circles, but it was celebrated in other circles: Henri Lefebvre captures this approach very well when he writes that it *"élabore et construit un objet théorique, un objet possible et cela à partir d'informations portant sur la réalité ainsi que d'une problématique posée par cette réalité. La transduction suppose un feedback incessant entre le cadre conceptuel utilisé et les observations empiriques ... Elle introduit la rigueur dans l'invention et la connaissance dans l'utopie"* (Lefebvre 1968: 121).

This approach has an experimental flavour, and is in the nature of serious play with a prototype, designed to help in *"l'exploration du possible humain avec l'aide de l'image et de*

---

[6] Courchene, *The Community of the Canadas* (1991), and Courchene and Powell, *A First Nations Province* (1992).

l'imaginaire, accompagnée d'une incessante référence à la problématique donnée dans le réel. L'utopie expérimentale déborde l'usage habituel de l'hypothèse dans les sciences sociales" (Lefebvre 1961: 192).

Courchene became even more ambitious in his Mabel Timlin Lecture at the University of Saskatchewan in 1999. This project – based on the explicit recognition that capital and technology can be obtained on the global scene, and that the fundamental asset Canada can really build on in the new information economy is its human capital – led Courchene to attempt a grandiose design of what Canada has to become in our information age – *a state of minds* (Courchene 2001). This baroque book tackles the most challenging task of defining how Canada must change, and what this change implies. This is a work of social architecture (Perlmutter 1965).

Courchene as social architect is not following in the footsteps of the austere Le Corbusier, but of the ebullient Frank Gehry. Reading Courchene's *A State of Minds* is not unlike exploring Gehry's Guggenheim Museum in Bilbao: there is a basic theme – human capital – but Courchene succeeds in bringing an extraordinary number of other dimensions and knowledge wedges to bear on his complex design for Canada. The multiple schemes he invokes give a Borgesian quality to the search for the underpinning or overriding organizing principle behind the plan: one that has been extracted by only very careful readers.

This might sound like an indictment – but only for those who are still absorbed by the bow-arrow-marksmanship antiquarian view of policy making. Courchene has not operated in this mode for quite some time. For Courchene (as for Perlmutter), "the social architect does not build the institution; the institution is built by the clients" (Perlmutter 1965: 32). His book only intended to set out the construction site: his insights were invitations for stakeholders to join the construction process. It was not a set of blueprints imposed from above, to be either executed by the state or followed religiously by journeymen. He was designing a collaborative exploratory venture.

In the same way as Courchene's mode of reasoning is unusual, his design thinking is also unusual. Once a sense of direction has been injected, he lets go: for him, the innovators he welcomes should not feel the need for constant supervision (Brown 2009: 74). Policy and strategy are no longer an intervention by *Big G (Government)* – hierarchical, centralized, authoritarian, coercive – pretending to have all the information, the power and the resources necessary to steer the social system in desired directions, but the result of *small g (governance)* – pluralist, participative, experimentalist – developing an inquiring system capable of ensuring adequate wayfinding and eliciting resilience and innovation.

We are no longer in *the ethereal world of leadership*, based on the assumption that someone has all the information, power and resources to ensure effective coordination, but in *the practical world of stewardship*, where no one is fully in charge, and power, resources and information are widely distributed among many hands and heads, where experiments nudge the system by fostering social learning (Paquet 2009).

Auspices, futuribles and the viewpoint from a crane

Over the last little while, Courchene has been even more daring. He has produced (among a large number of other works) some significantly broader and more encompassing pieces: for example, in 2011, a paper on nothing less than the rekindling of the American dream, and, in 2012, a distillation of the milestones or turning points in Canada's recent policy history.[7] These papers are in the nature of *map-making*: to develop the required vista, Tom Courchene uses the metaphor of a crane, lifting the observer so that, from an elevated perspective point, he can better see the landscape, and maybe even see a bit beyond the horizon (Normann 2001).

Courchene's ambition is not only to take stock, but to 'up-frame' – to redefine and expand the boundaries of the system he is looking at in space and time, in order to better gauge the

---

[7] Courchene's *Rekindling the American Dream – A Northern Perspective* (2011) and *Policy Signposts in Postwar Canada – Reflections of a Market Populist* (2012).

knowable unknown. From that perspective point, there is a simultaneous perception of emerging inconsistencies and the possibility of detecting what is actionable, what might be the joint enactment of a meaningful future.

While this work remains grounded in a good knowledge of the minutiae of the policy processes, in an unusual familiarity with the many-dimensional Canadian socio-political-economy as instituted process, and in an informed view of the world context, these last pieces of writing also reveal somewhat the *market populist cosmology* on which Courchene builds his concerns, conjectures and designs. Courchene stays clear of normative admonitions. But he does not shy away from showing his colours: a person who has a healthy respect for both the market and for the popular distrust of government and big business.

Courchene has no taste for self-analysis. He simply puts his views on the table so that all will know where he comes from, but he does not feel the need to defend them, nor to celebrate his cosmology and argue against alternative views even when they are questionable. This would lead him into confrontations, and this is not his style – at least not in the recent past. He is satisfied to leave to others such debates about epistemology, methodology, and the like.

On matters bordering on political philosophy in particular, such avoidances of confrontation are not necessarily ascribable to a single cause. It may be conjectured at times that it is by *esprit de corps* (for he remains a member of the 'Queen's tribe'), or as an echo effect of *bad memories* (of moments when he suffered brutal rebuffs for his radical statements about the effects of ill-inspired redistribution policies on regional disparities, or for his argument in favour of a North American monetary union), or as a result of *sheer congenital kindness*. However, whatever the source of his reluctance to unleash the enormous power of his critical thinking in 'arenas' where questionable positions are defended, he may have to shoulder some responsibility for having allowed these questionable positions to remain unchallenged.

For instance, Courchene is surprisingly uncritical in not exploring further the trade-off between pro-market populism and egalitarianism. In *Rekindling the American Dream,* he would appear to put on a par the faults of the dysfunctional American political system, and the reluctance of Americans to fall into the doldrums of egalitarianism (which is quite different from the pursuit of equality of opportunity) in explaining his bleak prospect for the rekindling of the American dream.[8] In the same manner, in *Policy Signposts in Postwar Canada,* Courchene as market populist presents a balanced clinical outlook on all issues, except when it comes to immigration and multiculturalism. On these latter issues, his kindness about the policies of the last few decades are, not only surprising, but appear to be unduly indulgent.[9]

Both these pieces are reflective in content and tone, and may be regarded as a pair of *hand-over memoranda* – the label used for the notes ambassadors hand to their successors upon leaving a post. They are also revealing in allowing us (however obliquely and hesitatingly) to peek at the market populist cosmology that has guided his work over the last few decades.

The new frontier for a market populist

Are these papers (as some have said) the "culmination" of Courchene's decades of policy work? I do not think so. These pieces could be a harbinger of his forays into a new territory.

---

[8] For a more persuasive market populist view on the US predicament, see Luigi Zingales, *A Capitalism for the People – Recapturing the Lost Genius of American Prosperity* (2012); for a more robust exposé of the perils of allowing the idea of the pursuit of equality of outcomes to taint ever so slightly the legitimate pursuit of equality of opportunity, see John Kekes, *The Illusions of Egalitarianism* (2003). On the first front, it is not so much sins of commission that one may blame Courchene for (since he has been clear about his focus on equality of opportunities and not equality of outcomes in some of this writings) but sins of omission – not critically and starkly denouncing positions building on much equivocation on those issues. In particular, Courchene uses the very word egalitarian in a way that is potentially misleading, since it has acquired an ideological flavour and has underpinned the defence of unrestricted entitlements to become an idea in good currency.

[9] For a contrarian view, see Gilles Paquet, *Moderato Cantabile: Toward principled governance for Canada's immigration regime* (2012).

Very few economists have taken any time to reflect on their craft in Canada. This has deprived *la relève* – the generations of newcomers to the profession – of much learning about what economics is all about – not as discipline, corporatism, cronyism and ideology – but as a burden of office, as a *métier*. This is probably why the political economy tradition is in danger of drying up in Canada: it has not been acknowledged enough, celebrated enough, remembered adequately, or explained sufficiently to the new generations.

The turn taken by economics over the last 40 years has all but obliterated much interest in economic history, the history of economic thought, and the meaning of the craft of economists as social critics, social architects, organizers and public intellectuals.

As a result of the shift from political economy (and its focus on content) to economics as discipline and method, most of the recent cohorts of economists have come to display an "unsettling or rash lack of concern" – the definition of criminal negligence in the Criminal Code – for the critical appraisal of the mental prisons and toxic ideologies that have plagued their house.

Courchene's determination to be non-confrontational in the face of some of those mental prisons and ideologies may have been costly. It may explain in part why so many of his very interesting and promising ideas have not been picked up. His imaginative new ways of doing things could not be easily grafted onto a basic structure that is crippled by the flawed principles and norms of the sort of economics in good currency – unless their foundations are challenged.

One might hope that Courchene can be persuaded that the time is ripe for him to reflect on the alternative foundational principles and norms on which his rather unique and particularly successful *corpus* of works as a political economist has been built.

It may no longer be sufficient to tackle some of the wicked problems of the day.

What is needed is a philosophical challenge of the conventional wisdom underpinning the institutional order and the paradigm in good currency. And only a Tom Courchene with his impeccable credentials as a diagnostician, social architect, organizer and public intellectual could tackle this Himalayan task: a task that only a true *savanturier* would be tempted to accept.

Conclusion

These are some of the questions Tom Courchene might ask:

• What might a market populist have to say about the ambient culture of entitlements, and radical egalitarianism?
• What would market-based ethics look like?

Tackling these sorts of questions would not only be timely, but it would also allow Courchene to develop more fully and clearly the unstated cosmology that has guided much of his work over the last 25 years, and to clarify once and for all some of the equivocal statements that may have crept into his voluminous writings as a result of his unwarranted kindness.

Setting the record straight does not mean necessarily simplifying. In fact, most of the time, it means complicating issues that have been too readily simplified.

References

Alinsky, Saul D. 1972. *Rules for Radicals – A Pragmatic Primer for Realistic Radicals.* New York, NY: Vintage Books.

Brown, Tim. 2009. *Change by Design.* New York, NY: HarperCollins.

Courchene, Thomas J. 1987. *Les offrandes des Rois mages – Etat-providence ou Etat-providentiel?* Scarborough, ON: C.D. Howe Institute.

Courchene, Thomas J. 1989. *What Does Ontario Want?* Toronto, ON: York University, Robarts Centre for Canadian Studies reprinted in Courchene, Thomas J. 1991. *Rearrangements – The Courchene Papers.* Oakville, ON: Mosaic Press, p. 1-42.

Courchene, Thomas J. 1991. *The Community of the Canadas.* Kingston, ON: Queen's University, Institute of Intergovernmental Relations.

Courchene Thomas J. 2001. *A State of Minds – Toward a Human Capital Future for Canadians.* Montreal, QC: Institute for Research on Public Policy.

Courchene Thomas J. 2011. *Rekindling the American Dream – A Northern Perspective.* Montreal, QC: Institute for Research on Public Policy.

Courchene Thomas J. 2012. *Policy Signposts in Postwar Canada – Reflections of a Market Populist.* Montreal, QC: Institute for Research on Public Policy.

Courchene, Thomas J. and L.M. Powell. 1992. *A First Nations Province.* Kingston, ON: Queen's University, Institute of Intergovernmental Relations.

Johnson, Harry G. 1968. "Canadian contributions to the discipline of economics," *Canadian Journal of Economics,* 1: 129-146.

Kekes, John. 2003. *The Illusions of Egalitarianism.* Ithaca, NY: Cornell University Press.

Lefebvre, Henri. 1961. "Utopie expérimentale: pour un nouvel urbanisme," *Revue Francaise de Sociologie,* 2 (July-September).

Lefebvre, Henri. 1968. *Le droit à la ville.* Paris, FR: Éditions Anthropos.

Leijonhufvud, Axel. 1973. "Life among the Econ," *Western Economic Journal,* 11(3): 327-337.

Neill, Robin F. and Gilles Paquet. 1993. "L'économie hérétique: Canadian economics before 1967," *Canadian Journal of Economics*, 26(1): 3-13.

Normann, Richard. 2001. *Reframing Business: When the Map Changes the Landscape*. Chichester, UK: John Wiley & Sons, Part V.

Paquet, Gilles. 2008. "Robert Bourassa, l'homme de Buridan" in G. Paquet, *Tableau d'avancement – Petite ethnographie interprétative d'un certain Canada français*. Ottawa, ON: University of Ottawa Press, p. 57-69.

Paquet, Gilles. 2009. "Stewardship versus Leadership" in G. Paquet, *Scheming Virtuously: The Road to Collaborative Governance*. Ottawa, ON: Invenire Books, p. 97-116.

Paquet, Gilles. 2012. *Moderato Cantabile: Toward principled governance for Canada's immigration regime*. Ottawa, ON: Invenire Books.

Perlmutter, Howard V. 1965. *Toward a Theory and Practice of Social Architecture – The Building of Indispensable Institutions*. London, UK: Tavistock.

Romme. A. Georges L. 2003. "Making a Difference: Organization as Design," *Organization Science*, 14(5): 558-573.

Schrage, Michael. 2000. *Serious Play: How the World's Best Companies Simulate to Innovate*. Boston, MA: Harvard Business School Press.

Sen, Amartya. 1999. "Galbraith and the Art of Description" in H. Sassoon (ed.). *Between Friends: Perspectives on John Kenneth Galbraith*. Boston, MA: Houghton-Mifflin, p. 139-145.

Zingales, Luigi. 2012. *A Capitalism for the People – Recapturing the Lost Genius of American Prosperity*. New York, NY: Basic Books.

CONCLUSION

| On Synthesis and Reasonableness

"The part always has a tendency to unite with the whole,
in order to escape its imperfection ..."
Leonardo da Vinci

Preamble

umans are creatures of habit. Once habituated, they cling to an often reductive and misleading *manière de voir* that they have stumbled on by happenstance and that they have become accustomed to. They do so even when the context has changed, and the perspective in good currency no longer provides a useful lens to make sense of the new realities. Any organizational deviant may be the vital link to a newer and more adequate paradigm in the making, but that will never make the organization value the deviant. As Warren Bennis put it, "most organizations would rather risk obsolescence than make room for the non-conformists in their midst" (1976: 40).

The same holds for *views of the 'lifeworld.'* They develop over a long time and tend to crystallize in ways that become difficult to modify, even when they have become antiquated. The power of cognitive dissonance and groupthink, in the face of emerging realities that one does not feel comfortable with, is immense.

The resistance to new conceptual frameworks and to new images of the 'lifeworld' tends to slow social learning, and even stunt its progress. The proclivity to maintain inadequate frames of reference and descriptions of the context, despite evidence to the contrary, triggers feats of rationalization and clever intellectual gymnastics in defence of the earlier views. Indeed, one of the sleekest devices is to inappropriately invoke Ockham's razor, and to argue that the new approach is a concatenation of arguments that are unduly complex and difficult to understand and, therefore, cannot hope to displace the less complex and more mundane form of argument supporting the original position.

Obviously, some things are difficult to understand. But most of what one finds difficult to understand cannot be ascribed to such absolute difficulty. Most of the time, things are found difficult to understand because they do not fit well with the puzzled person's frame of reference. This is so because grappling with them would force him/her to reconsider a fair number of assumptions and beliefs that are dearly held, and force him/her to work hard at mastering the new ways.

Dynamic conservatism, as Donald Schön (1971: chapter 2) would call it, and a certain intellectual laziness and *insouciance* are at the foundation of many of the learning disabilities explored earlier in this book. So it is not entirely possible to escape from dealing with these predicaments if one is trying to distil practical advice to overcome these learning disabilities.

In this conclusion, I proceed in two stages.

First, in a succinct way, I remind the reader that we live in chaotic times, marked by discontinuities. The ground is in motion, many of the reference points in use evolve and, at times, even traditional guideposts of necessity cease to be of relevance. Such discontinuous change requires discontinuous thinking, even upside-down thinking.

In the same way as the Copernican revolution displaced the Ptolemaic framework, pretense that anyone has all the information, power and resources necessary to be fully in charge in most of our modern socio-economic-political systems (i.e., Big G governing) has been debunked (Paquet

2013a). It has been replaced by a small g governance framework that suggests that power, resources and information are widely distributed, and that effective coordination has to be crafted. In the same manner as the Quantum revolution that replaced the Newtonian view of a system of mechanical and predictable objects by one where contradiction and unpredictability reign, and where it is often impossible to determine cause and effect except in probabilistic terms, governance has shattered the myth of common and shared values, and argued that a blending of perspectives is necessary to generate some workable guidance in wayfinding (Paquet and Wilson 2011).

Second, a case is made for two new levers/guideposts in this complex, turbulent and chaotic world: the case for *synthesis* as an essential addendum to a toolbox crowded by an analytical instrumentation, and the case for *reasonableness* as a broader and sounder appreciative system than the sole reliance on instrumental rationality.

This second stage may appear to some as unnecessary, but such a view is rather naïve. Over the last century, analysis and instrumental rationality have dominated the scene so thoroughly that they have fundamentally displaced and marginalized other perspectives and approaches, such as ecological rationality and contextual fit (Smith 2008). Synthesis as the reference point on method, and reasonableness as the reference point on substance must be forcefully promoted, otherwise both may continue to be unduly overshadowed by their toxic competitors.

On the basis of these more integrative and comprehensive notions, I reflect in closing on what challenges must be confronted by the perplexed in the design of less ineffective inquiring systems (both in terms of substance and method) as a way to ensure less ineffective governance.

Cautious and modest are the operative words when it comes to concluding in such matters. For one is constrained by the very *imprecise* nature of governance (Paquet 2013b), and by the impossibility for our reflections to generate conclusions that would be general, simple and precise – some trade-offs apply.[1]

Blending of perspectives in a chaotic age

The expression "the age of unreason" used by Charles Handy (1990) is a useful shorthand way to connote times that are both chaotic, and difficult to grasp with the usual toolbox of instrumental rationality. It emphasizes both the complexity and strange dynamics:

- of the *unpredictable change* of an external environment, subject to black swan phenomena and avalanches, *à la* Taleb (2007), and
- of the *wickedness* of the internal organizational environment, where there would not appear to be agreement on objectives or goals pursued (since stakeholders have different perspectives and objectives), and little certainty and stability in the means-ends relationships (Rittel and Webber 1973).

This broad *tohu-bohu* has triggered a dramatic transformation of the notion of governing. In a world where information, power and resources are widely distributed in many heads and hands, and where stakeholders have different cosmologies, nobody is truly in charge, and *stewardship* – a more integrative term that emerges from network collaborative governance – replaces the more anthropomorphic and individualistic term *leadership* (Paquet 2009: chapter 5).

This sort of emergent and groping wayfinding requires a significant use of *blending* – a generative cognitive operation that produces a conceptual structure not provided by the particular perspectives that serve as inputs in the blend. Blending generates new integrative viewpoints, but only partly on the basis of the old partial ones, and serves a variety of cognitive purposes: triggering ideas, arguments and

---

[1] As suggested by Thorngate (1976) and Weick (1979), a model cannot be simple, general and precise. If on the face of a clock, General is at noon, Precise is at four o'clock, and Simple is at eight o'clock; a model can only emphasize one characteristic to the detriment of the others. By choosing to be mainly general, one must accept to be less precise and simple.

inferences developed in the blend, with effects on cognition (Turner 2001).

Blending contributes not only to the enrichment of perspectives, but also to the reconciliation of the diverse viewpoints held by various stakeholders.

There are three operations in the construction of the blend: *composition, completion,* and *elaboration.* These three operations create the new emergent mental space of the blend. Composition provides the new frame of reference, and relationships that did not exist in the particular perspectives; completion draws from the background knowledge to complete the pattern; elaboration develops the blend through imaginative mental exploration. The most interesting aspect of blending is obviously elaboration – the imaginative extension of whatever space has ensued to generate a dynamic blend with a life of its own, capable of carrying the argument further.

A provisional blend can guide the learning process toward ways out of wicked problem situations in a complex adaptive system that encompasses institutional, epistemic and moral dimensions. This interacting and evolving set of individuals and groups, bound together (but at the same time kept apart) by structures, technologies and theories has certain features: (1) it is *open* to its environment; (2) it must *adapt* to its environment through modifications and differentiation; and (3) this generates systems of interaction so complex that agents cannot analyze them *ex ante* but must simply adapt, and discover new rules that generate coordination and integration – as they proceed.

Taking advantage of these organic and emergent forces means embracing complexity and fully acknowledging our ignorance. This entails recognizing the futility of massive mechanical interventions in an unpredictable world, and the centrality of *bricolage* and small interventions to modify the actors' different settings and time horizons – in order to accelerate the process of social learning, to tinker with interaction patterns by modifying proximity and creating shared space or forums, by sharpening performance measurements, and helping to catalyze a better selection of agents and strategies.[2]

Synthesis as conduit, and reasonableness as guidepost

Much of what has been discussed above conveys the strong message that one cannot fix organizations unless one fixes the system.

Yet, as Lant Pritchett explains in his discussion of schools (and therefore of education systems), most of us are worthless at thinking about system problems because "the number of times any of us needs to understand systems is vanishingly small" (Pritchett 2013: 140ff). We need a great deal of thinking about objects and agents in our daily life, and we are incredibly sophisticated about them. In contrast, we are incredibly unsophisticated about systems.

As a result, when people do think about systems, they extrapolate their expertise in objects and agents to systems, and anthropomorphize them: they tell stories about systems as if the system were an agent. This is because they much prefer people explanations than system explanations.

Organizations are complex adaptive systems and are not agents. They can have an outcome that no agent of the system intended – an emergent outcome that one cannot make sense of without an understanding of what the system is about, of what processes underpin it, of how it works and evolves in ways that are not necessarily simple, or linear, or predictable. Therefore, developing an appreciation of an organization as a system entails not being satisfied with a snapshot of one of its dimensions, but developing an appreciation of the nexus of forces that underpin its dynamics – something that cannot be accomplished without blending many approaches to many of its dimensions.

[2] For a more elaborate discussion of this approach in the case of sustainability, see Gilles Paquet, *Tackling Wicked Policy Problems: Equality, Diversity, and Sustainability* (2013c), chapter 6.

Two blending efforts (among many) in systems thinking may be singled out as particularly important in the sort of exploration based on critical thinking and the construction of inquiring systems that I praised earlier: *the blending of perspectives* to transcend the myopic tyranny of reductive analytical modes, and *the blending/reconciliation of the agonistic tensions* among the different agents and groups with quite different views of the world in order to generate a broader and more encompassing appreciative system than the one rooted in the instrumental rationality of particular agents or groups.

(a) As Valerie Brown puts it, the dominant form of Western culture shines brightly on individualism, competition, hierarchy and analytical thinking. Tools for synthesis-based thinking, collaborative inquiry, and integrative governance lie in the shadows (Brown 2008). This analytical bent has led to efforts to 'solve' problems by slicing issue domains into smaller segments where simple formal cause-effect and instrumental rationality relations can be more easily isolated. This has fuelled a representation of the world as a fractured and disjointed cosmology, characterized by local zones of instrumental rationality and certainty. In this manner, disciplines have emerged as the dominant lenses that were based on rigorous axiomatic systems, and claimed to be able to deduce what forms institutions and organizations should have, from their partial but supposedly universal principles.

Disciplines are anchored in very narrow conceptions of humans, and in very reductive methods of inquiry – ignoring all sorts of dimensions of concrete realities and all sorts of knowledge in order to obtain tractability in some narrow sense, and promoting methods of inquiry that are less comprehensive and practical than they should be.

This is because the usual analytical inquiries rely on silo-like approaches, and neglect both the blending of perspectives held by the different stakeholders, and the taking into account of untraded interdependencies among the different groups that are so important in the processes of collaboration. In that sense, synthesis, while maintaining the advantages of specialized inquiry, wishes to find ways:

- to develop synoptic perspectives by combining and blending different points of view on any given theme;
- to reclaim the capacity to reconnect contributors to a whole, and develop a synergy by constructive interactions;
- to generate both a fresh whole from unit parts, and integrative thinking capable of constructive collective decisions (open-ended, future-directed, etc.); and
- to nudge successful change as a result of parts becoming active parts of an effective whole.

By ensuring that integrative thinking is given its proper place (which should be large), new ways of scoping the context, new principles, and new tools will emerge. Synthesis is an approach that tries to find a way back to the whole, to put Humpty Dumpty somewhat back together.

(b) The comprehensiveness of perspectives generated by a more synoptic view is bound to produce an appreciation that goes much beyond the narrow ambit of the rationalist ideology and its dreams of a universal method, a perfect language, and a unitary system (Toulmin 2001).[3] As Stephen Toulmin puts it, "philosophical dreams are soap bubbles. Taken at face value they may deceive us; but handled roughly they vanish" (*Ibid*.: 69). Much of the last century has lived under the theoretical charm of rationalism, but *de facto*, in the trenches, what has emerged is a process of inquiry that has had to proceed in a zigzag fashion – in an interaction of some rationalist forays with empiricist inquiries that fed on one another in search, not for *characteristica universalis*, but for a promising language of inquiry likely to generate effective stewardship and

---

[3] For a caustic criticism of these dreams, see chapter 5 in Stephen Toulmin, *Return to Reason*, 2001.

wayfinding (i.e., ways that satisfy more than standards of logical coherence (Vickers 1965)).

Much of the work produced by the traditional approaches to policy research has fallen into the rationalist trap, and focused on stylized and quite unrealistic attempts to falsify hypotheses about some objective reality, according to the canons of scientific experimentation. This is too narrow a focus for policy research and action hypotheses in turbulent times. I have sketched in chapter 2 above some elements for the construction of a broader and more comprehensive approach (in the spirit of Friedmann-Abonyi) built on reasonableness, rather than trying to build on narrow instrumental rationality at the core of the inquiry and stewardship system.

This is the sort of apparatus required to comprehensively explore the scene of the wicked problems that result from complexity and uncertainty. This is also the sort of framework that senior executives need to use in order to approach the sort of challenges they face in our modern socio-economies: searching for responses that are not only technically feasible, but also socially acceptable, not too politically destabilizing, and practically implementable with the help of partners.

Toulmin makes a powerful call to redress the balance between the narrow instrumental rationality imperatives and the reasonableness imperatives. He argues for a need to confront the challenge of an uncertain and unpredictable world, not with inflexible ideologies and abstract theories, but by returning to a more humane and compassionate form of reason, one that accepts the diversity and complexity that is human nature as an essential beginning for all intellectual inquiry (Toulmin 2001).

This is the sort of roadmap proposed by Valerie Brown and her consorts in Australia, especially in discussions of problems of sustainability (Brown et al. 2010). However, not all work on this front is so focused. Much of the probing in good currency can only be regarded as window dressing around the notion of network governance, or as some thinly disguised defence of old style leadership, under labels falsely promising ways of 'tackling wicked problems.'[4]

Four challenges

It should be clear that synthesis and reasonableness are no panaceas. They may serve at best, as we suggest above, as conduit and guidepost. They are likely to be most helpful, in an oblique way, in meeting the four major challenges that I have hinted at throughout this volume.

The first challenge is to refurbish the process of critical thinking, and to improve the inquiring systems in use. On this front, much can be learned from a greater awareness of the potentialities of blending, à la Mark Taylor, from the experience of Valerie A. Brown and her associates in Australia with a greater emphasis on synthesis, and from the development of the sort of approach to collaborative governance that has emerged from the work at the Centre on Governance at the University of Ottawa (Hubbard, Paquet and Wilson 2012).

The second challenge is to exorcize all the sources of toxicity that have infested the processes of knowledge acquisition and of collaboration over the last while. I have drawn attention to only a few of these pathologies in this volume, but there are many more. Recently (Paquet and Ragan 2012), a number of major interfaces and zones of tension within organizations were examined (X-inefficiencies at the management-labour interface, escaping fault at the value-adding matrix interface, externalities at the socio-physical environment interface, hijacking at the governance interface, and moral relativism at the interface of the organization and its social and moral contexts) that were shown to be the loci of important sources of pathologies and dysfunctions. These pathologies were shown to be potentially corrected, in part, by modifications to certain

---

[4] This variegated literature seems to be most reluctant to abandon the language of leadership (with all its baggage) and consequently has generated much confusion in allowing the impression that wicked policy problems could be tackled through the traditional approaches if those were slightly adjusted – Goldsmith and Eggers, *Governing by Networks*, 2004 and Nickerson and Sanders (eds.), *Tackling Wicked Government Problems*, 2013.

necessary incentive reward systems, but additionally through developing conventions of trust and other moral contracts. Much more critical thinking must be brought to bear on these organizational failures, ascribable to ideological, behavioural and organizational blockages.

The third challenge has to do with the need for a more encompassing outlook on the socio-economic scene in order to enrich the appreciation system, and in so doing, make it likely that one will be able to improve the social learning process, the stewarding process, and the wayfinding process.

This need for novel, more open, and more encompassing perspectives must act as a forceful motivation to develop *cranes* (to use the language of Richard Normann (2001: Part V)) which send down a hook to lift the observer into a position where new realms are visible that could not be imagined from aground, allowing a broader and richer perspective. These cranes should (1) *broaden* our perspective to take into account interactions (social domain), mind frames (cognitive domain), and ecological and power interfaces; (2) *lengthen* our time horizon to take into account a more extended future and the possibility of learning our way out of predicaments; and (3) *elevate* our perspective point to take into account the common public culture within which meso-organizations are nested, and even what is beyond the contingent aspects of the lives of partners in organizations – the transcendent.

There is no standard blueprint for crane construction, but some principles have been proposed by Normann to meet the challenge of designing useful cranes. The crane must be capable of:

- taking stock of the context and of the mega-community;
- up-framing, i.e., redefining the out-boundaries of the system one is in;
- moving boldly into future scenarios;
- aiding in wind-tunneling any prototypes that may emerge; and
- signaling the sort of improved competences, collaboration, and organization design improvements required.

Chapter 5 has been a fairly modest exercise in developing a crane to look at the Canadian *malaise*, and has proposed the revival of the idea of a Committee on the Long Run – originally proposed to the Royal Society of Canada in 1987 (Braybrooke and Paquet 1987). But much more ambitious schemes have been elaborated of late, and have been carried out with gusto. For instance, a most interesting and ambitious one has been developed by the Oxford Martin School at the University of Oxford.[5]

The fourth challenge is the development of a *design attitude*: for, as we explained in Paquet and Ragan (2012), it will be necessary if the focus of efforts in the future is to be on exploration leading to the redesign of organizations and institutions, to ensure not only better performance, but also (and most importantly) to improve social learning. Such exploration leads to learning by doing, and "involves inquiry into systems that do not yet exist" (Romme 2003: 558). This, in turn, requires a new way of thinking: *design thinking* (Brown 2009).

This is a way of thinking that escapes groupthink and convergent thinking, which are designed to *make* choices, and favours divergent thinking, designed to *create* choices. The focus of the inquiry shifts from the *exploitation* of existing knowledge to *exploration* for new knowledge: a shift from routine management to the continuous reinvention of the organization, from a refining of arrangements in place to exploration based as much on intuition as analysis, and a shift from short term and low risk to long term and high risk undertakings (March 1991; Martin 2009).

This new way of thinking builds on experimentation, prototyping and serious play, and makes the highest and best use of grappling, grasping, discerning and sense-making as part of reflective generative learning. It bypasses the simple use of focus groups and surveys as rearview mirrors into the future. Design thinking is a systematic approach to innovation: not

---

[5] The stellar composition of the Oxford Martin Commission for Future Generations and its impressive report, *Now for the Long Term*, October 2013, would appear to make it a template for such future initiatives.

being satisfied with managing existing offerings and adapting to new users, but creating new offerings for new users (Brown 2009: 261).

This sort of development is no longer simply a vague idea. Considerable attention has been given to operationalizing such work on the craft of stewardship. A most fascinating example is the study done by the Helsinki Design Lab that has not only experimented with a design approach, but has published both some guidelines for systemic change, and some case studies about the craft of stewardship (Boyer, Cook and Steinberg 2011, 2013).

Coda

The first two parts of this book highlighted some difficulties associated with the waning of critical thinking, the crudeness of the inquiring systems at the core of the stewardship of our organizations, but also with the mental prisons and the blockages to collaboration in the social learning process that is necessary to ensure effective coordination, resilience and innovation in modern organizations. Obliquely, these difficulties have indicated the sort of directions in which one would have to work to repair the organization failures that have of necessity ensued.

Part III has also indicated ways in which one might proceed to overcome these difficulties – through a diagnostic paper on the Canadian *malaise*, and a short excursus on the work of Tom Courchene, a Canadian social scientist who has probed the Canadian scene most critically over the last few decades, and has worked creatively at redesigning organizations and institutions that gave signs of being in need of repair.

In conclusion, some guideposts and some challenges have been identified on the way forward.

All this has been presented more or less matter-of-factly. Moreover, there have been sufficient indications of the gravity of the situation, and of the general directions in which it is necessary to proceed to effect the sort of repairs required, that a person of good will might be expected to be nudged into taking some action to improve the situation.

But this diagnosis is overly optimistic.

It is not that Canadians are not well aware of these trends, pathologies and blockages, but they have developed such a tolerance to these factors, and such a sense that they cannot do much about them, that fatalism has taken hold. In order to live not too uncomfortably with these trends, they have simply chosen not to think too much about it. Over time, insensitivity to these phenomena has developed, and with this, toxic impacts. Consequently, corrective action is unlikely to be triggered organically in normal times.

Given this burden of inertia and anomie, many have come to believe that no major overhauling can be expected unless some catastrophe generates a rude awakening. Some call for the arrival on the scene of a modern-day Cassandra. But it should be remembered that, even though Cassandra was right, nobody believed her! Others would settle for stratagems like 'catastrophisme éclairé' à la Dupuy – a ruse to deceive society into taking seriously the omens of disaster that would normally be ignored. Such deceit is unlikely to work and is morally reprehensible (Dupuy 2002).

We are facing a cultural crisis that cannot be resolved by a sleight of hand, but by a cultural change. The Canadian *malaise* has been the result of a quiet cultural capitulation; overcoming it may require nothing more or less than a quiet cultural renaissance. This cannot be accomplished without the restoration of a *culture of responsibility* and *a culture of mindfulness.*

- A culture of responsibility is a culture that encourages responsible behaviour, in which not only *people* bear responsibility for their action – a system like the Romans had, where if you built a bridge, you stood under the arch when the scaffolding was removed – but in which it is also widely recognized that any *organization* where it is easy to steal or cheat is perverse, and perpetrating a great moral injury on the people who work there (Larcker and Tayan 2014).

- A culture of mindfulness is a culture geared to improving sensitivity, the capacity to react quickly to the unexpected, and the capacity to contain the toxic impacts of these unexpected avalanches. This has been synthesized by Weick and Sutcliffe (2007) as entailing, particularly in daily life, such things as preoccupation with failure, reluctance to unduly simplify things, closeness to operations, commitment to resilience, etc. This is the sort of attitude observed in high-reliability organizations.

As Ortega y Gasset said, "life is fired at us point-blank" (Gasset 1957: 41) – it may not be possible to predict the tipping point events that might initiate moves in the direction of that sort of revolution in the mind. However slender the opening, or the leverage it would appear to provide, any opportunity to promote responsibility and mindfulness is an opportunity that cannot be ignored.

It is the burden of office of all active citizens – and all citizens should be active citizens – to work at this restoration, for even though there is no guarantee that any particular move will be the beginning of a groundswell on the way to cultural change, there is no assurance that it will not.

In the words of Fritz Schumacher, "the art of living is always to make a good thing out of a bad thing". This would appear to proceed in two stages: first, recognizing that "we have actually descended into *infernal regions*", and summoning "the courage and imagination needed for a *turning around*, a *metanoia* ... [and] seeing the world in a new light, namely, as a place where the things modern man continuously talks about and always fails to accomplish can *actually be done*" (Schumacher 1977: 139).

This explains why I am not hopeful, but I have hope.

References

Bennis, Warren. 1976. *The Unconscious Conspiracy.* New York, NY: Amacon.

Boyer, Bryan, Justin W. Cook and Marco Steinberg. 2011. *Recipes for Systemic Change.* Helsinki: SITRA Helsinki Design Lab.

Boyer, Bryan, Justin W. Cook and Marco Steinberg. 2013. *Legible Practices – Six Stories about the Craft of Stewardship.* Helsinki: SITRA Helsinki Design Lab.

Braybrooke, David and Gilles Paquet. 1987, "Human Dimensions of Global Change: The Challenge to the Humanities and the Social Sciences," *Transactions of the Royal Society of Canada,* Fourth Series, Vol. XXV, p. 269-291.

Brown, Tim. 2009. *Change by Design.* New York, NY: HarperCollins.

Brown, Valerie A. 2008. *Leonardo's Vision – A guide to collective thinking and action.* Rotterdam, NL: Sense Publishers.

Brown, Valerie A. et al. (eds.). 2010. *Tackling Wicked Problems – Through the Transdisciplinary Imagination.* New York, NY: Earthscan.

Dupuy, Jean-Pierre. 2002. *Pour un catastrophisme éclairé – Quand l'impossible est certain.* Paris, FR: Seuil.

Friedmann, John and George Abonyi. 1976. "Social Learning: A Model for Policy Research," *Environment and Planning,* A8(8): 927-940.

Gasset, Ortega y. 1957. *Man and People [El hombre y la gente],* translated by Willard R. Trask.

Goldsmith, Stephen and William D. Eggers. 2004. *Governing by Network.* Washington, DC: The Brookings Institution Press.

Handy, Charles. 1990. *The Age of Unreason.* London, UK: Arrow Books.

Hubbard Ruth, Gilles Paquet and Christopher Wilson. 2012. *Stewardship.* Ottawa, ON: Invenire Books.

Larcker, David F. and Bryan Tayan. 2014. *Corporate Governance According to Charles T. Munger.* Stanford, CA: Rock Center for Corporate Governance.

March, James G. 1991. "Exploration and Exploitation in Organizational Learning," *Organization Science,* 2: 71-87.

Martin, Roger. 2009. *The Design of Business.* Boston, MA: Harvard Business School Press.

Nickerson, Jackson and Ronald Sanders (eds.). 2013. *Tackling Wicked Government Problems: A Practical Guide for Developing Enterprise Leaders.* Washington, DC: The Brookings Institution Press.

Normann, Richard. 2001. *Reframing Business: When the Map Changes the Landscape.* Chichester, UK: John Wiley & Sons.

Oxford Martin Commission for Future Generations. 2013. *Now for the Long Term.* Oxford, UK: University of Oxford, Oxford Martin School, October.

Paquet, Gilles. 2009. "Stewardship versus Leadership" in G. Paquet, *Scheming Virtuously: The Road to Collaborative Governance.* Ottawa, ON: Invenire Books, p. 97-116.

Paquet, Gilles. 2013a. "Governance as Mythbuster," *www. optimumonline.ca,* 43(1): 23-35.

Paquet, Gilles. 2013b. "La gouvernance, science de l'imprécis," *Organisations & Territoires,* 21(3): 5-17.

Paquet, Gilles. 2013c. *Tackling Wicked Policy Problems: Equality, Diversity, and Sustainability.* Ottawa, ON: Invenire Books.

Paquet, Gilles and Tim Ragan. 2012. *Through the Detox Prism: Exploring Organizational Failures and Design Responses.* Ottawa, ON: Invenire Books.

Paquet, Gilles and Christopher Wilson. 2011. "Collaborative Co-governance as Inquiring Systems," *www.optimumonline.ca,* 41(2): 1-12.

Pritchett, Lant. 2013. *The Rebirth of Education*. Washington, DC: Center for Global Development.

Rittel, Horst W.J. and Melvin M. Webber. 1973. "Dilemmas in a General Theory of Planning," *Policy Sciences*, (4): 156-169.

Romme. A. Georges L. 2003. "Making a Difference: Organization as Design," *Organization Science*, 14(5): 558-573.

Schön Donald A. 1971. *Beyond the Stable State*. New York, NY: Norton.

Schumacher Ernst F. 1977. *A Guide for the Perplexed*. New York, NY: Harper & Row.

Smith, Vernon L. 2008. *Rationality in Economics*. Cambridge, UK: Cambridge University Press.

Taleb, Nassim N. 2007. *The Black Swan – The Impact of the Highly Improbable*. New York, NY: Random House.

Thorngate, W. 1976. "'In General' vs. 'It Depends': Some Comments on the Gergen-Schlenker Debate," *Personality and Social Psychology Bulletin* 2, p. 404-410.

Toulmin, Stephen. 2001. *Return to Reason*. Cambridge, MA: Harvard University Press.

Turner, Mark. 2001. *Cognitive Dimensions of Social Science*. Oxford, UK: Oxford University Press.

Vickers, Geoffrey. 1965. *The Art of Judgment – A Study of Policy-Making*. London, UK: Chapman & Hall.

Weick, Karl E. 1979. *The Social Psychology of Organizing*. Reading, MA: Addison-Wesley.

Weick, Karl E. and Kathleen M. Sutcliffe. 2007 (2nd ed.). *Managing the Unexpected – Resilient Performance in an Age of Uncertainty*. New York, NY: John Wiley & Sons.

| Sources

Some segments of this book have been previously published or presented to public audiences in a slightly different form.

Chapter 1 was originally presented to a workshop at the Graduate School of Public and International Affairs of the University of Ottawa on November 19, 2013, and was subsequently published in 2014 in a different form in June 2014 in *www.optimumonline.ca*, 44(2).

Chapter 3 was originally published in 2009 in *www. optimumonline.ca*, 39(1): 14-27.

Chapter 4 was originally published in 2010 in *www. optimumonline.ca*, 40(1): 23-47.

Chapter 5 was originally published in 2013 in *www. optimumonline.ca*, 43(2): 1-12.

Chapter 6 was originally presented at a conference in celebration of Thomas J. Courchene held at Queen's University in Kingston, in October 2012. It will be published in a book at McGill-Queen's University Press in 2015.

Titles in the Collaborative Decentred Metagovernance Series

Other titles published by INVENIRE